Know
Senses

MARTIN WARNER

MOREHOUSE PUBLISHING
A Continuum imprint
www.morehousepublishing.com

Morehouse
4775 Linglestow Road, Harrisburg, PA 17112

Continuum
The Tower Building, 11 York Road, London SE1 7NX

Morehouse is an imprint of Continuum Books

www.continuumbooks.com

First published 2004

British Library Cataloguing-in-Publication Data
A catalogue record for this book is available from the British Library.

ISBN 0-8192-8109-3

Typeset by Kenneth Burnley in Wirral, Cheshire
Printed and bound in Great Britain by
Antony Rowe Ltd, Chippenham, Wiltshire

Contents

Introduction

What you have come to is *nothing* known to the senses
... But what you have come to is Mount Zion and the
city of the living God, the heavenly Jerusalem.

(Hebrews 12.18, 22, NJB)

A question about the mountain

The title of this book comes from the letter to the Hebrews.
At the culmination of that magnificent sweep of sacred
history the author describes heaven itself, the goal and
destination of the Christian pilgrimage.

Perhaps it is symbolic that the text with which the
description of this goal begins is ambiguous. The New
Revised Standard Version offers the translation, 'You have
not come to something that can be touched.' The older
translations follow a Greek text that requires us to read the
thing that cannot be touched or known to the senses as the
'mountain'.

Location on a mountain is a familiar context for revela-
tion of the mystery of God. Abraham and the sacrifice of
Isaac on the mountain in the land of Moriah, Moses on
Mount Sinai, and Elijah in the cave on Horeb; the mountain
of God; all foreshadow in some way the transfiguration of
Jesus on mount Tabor.

The significance of a mountain-top is that it is a place of
liminality. There one stands at a boundary, expressed in

some respects by the extent of human skill and courage required to get there, or the experience of remoteness and isolation. Immediately the senses are engaged. It may be in hunger and thirst, in the touch of flesh against ice and stone, in hearing silence, seeing the whole earth, or the sweat and smell of fear and exhaustion.

The senses and beyond

But the senses can guide us only so far in this experience. In the metaphor of religious experience we would say that God calls us to travel beyond the summit of sensory perception in order to experience the ever-greater character of Godself.

In this book we explore the ways in which each sense might lead us distinctively into a deeper understanding of the journey through Holy Week to Calvary and Easter Day. This also brings us to the boundaries of perception and understanding that require us to leave sense behind if we are to be brought to perfection through the paschal mystery of our redemption. Perhaps the most obvious example of this in Christian experience is that of St Paul, who is blinded by a vision, and in the darkness of having no sight is led across the boundary of what, for him, had not been credible: faith in Jesus Christ.

In all instances, our fullest participation in the events of Holy Week will draw us into encounter with God, through the experience of our senses but also through the challenge to leave them behind. It is like diving into the sea: a new world emerges in which we feel strange and unfamiliar with what governs it and how we inhabit it.

How to use this book

The book links each of the five senses with one of the days of Holy Week, and with Easter Day. These five chapters could provide the starting point for a Lent study group, and material for group discussion is included at the end of each chapter. There is also material for reflection at an individual level, and some of that could be used by a group.

My recollection of Lent books and courses in a parish was that we often missed a bit out, because of not starting on the days that follow Ash Wednesday. A five-fold division may, therefore, be useful. However, some people may want a sixth meeting or portion of material to read, and that makes possible something very useful, perhaps at the beginning of Lent.

The nature of our lectionary and public reading of the scriptures does not permit the reading of a whole book of the Bible at one go, or of serious portions of it that recount a complete cycle of stories, such as the Joseph cycle, or that of David, for example.

The Passion narratives form the most coherent sections of the four Gospels. You might choose to read the whole of one of them, or an Old Testament cycle of stories, and assess its internal and distinctive drama. You might choose to watch a film version, or listen to a musical one.

There might also be some other event that draws on our senses that you could visit. Art exhibitions, such as Bill Viola's 'The Passions' or 'Presence', sponsored by the Bible-lands charity, have provided excellent material for reflection.

I hope that some suggestions offered here might be of encouragement in the keeping of Lent and preparation for Easter. I hope that they might also be stimulating in the continuing search for knowledge of God through the many media of revelation and their use in our proclamation of the gospel.

This book comes out of the experience of being invited over the past three years to conduct an ordination retreat in the Diocese of Durham, preach during Holy Week in the Old St Pancras Team, Camden Town, London, and conduct a retreat for Healthcare Chaplains at the Royal Foundation of St Katherine, Limehouse, London. All three experiences were a huge privilege and I wish to record my profound gratitude for the invitations, from Bishop Michael Turnbull, Fr Nicholas Wheeler, and Fr Edward Lewis.

The task of jotting down my thoughts from those engagements and turning them into this book is one in which I have been encouraged and guided by a number of colleagues and friends, for whose wisdom, support and patience I am also very grateful. Among them are Robin Baird-Smith and Ben Hayes at Continuum, Stephen Cottrell, Rachel Boulding, Jim Walters, Rob Marshall, John Booth, Lyle Dennen, Hilary Pearson, Robert Mackley, Jamie Hawkey, David Rouch, Claire Foster and my other colleagues at St Paul's.

The suggestion that this book might make some contribution to the preparation for *Stand up for Jesus* (the event planned for Eastertide 2005 to mark the 150th anniversary of the founding of the Society of the Holy Cross) came, I think, from the Master of the Society of the Holy Cross, Fr David Houlding. His courtesy, wise counsel and gracious good humour are widely recognized and appreciated in many forums of the life of the Church of England. I dedicate this book to him as a statement of the respect and gratitude that so many have for his ministry.

Martin Warner
The Feast of the Transfiguration, 2004

Acknowledgements

'The Burial of the Dead' from *The Wasteland* in *Collected Poems 1909–1962* by T. S. Eliot, used with permission of Faber and Faber Ltd.

Streets of London by Ralph McTell, © 1970 Westminster Music Ltd, Suite 2.07, Plaza 535, Kings Road, London SW10 0SZ. International copyright secured. All rights reserved. Used by permission.

The English translation of the form for inscribing the paschal candle from 'Rite of Holy Week', © 1972, International Committee on English in the Liturgy, Inc. All rights reserved.

Extracts from the *Book of Common Prayer* (BCP), the rights in which are vested in the Crown, are reproduced by permission of the Crown's Patentee, Cambridge University Press.

Scripture quotations from the *New Revised Standard Version of the Bible*, © 1989 by the Division of Christian Education of the National Council of Churches of Christ in the USA. All rights reserved.

The poem 'Rublev' by Rowan Williams is reproduced with the permission of the author.

Extracts from *The Way* are reproduced with permission from the Editors.

Prayers for use in Lent

Take, Lord, all my liberty.
Receive my memory, and my whole will.
Whatever I have and possess, you have given me;
to you I restore it wholly,
and to your will I utterly surrender it for my direction.
Give me the love of you only, with your grace,
and I am rich enough, nor do I ask anything besides. Amen.
                                    (Prayer of St Ignatius of Loyola)

Pilgrim God, bless us with courage
    where our way is fraught with danger.
Bless us with good companions
    where the way demands a common cause.
Bless us with humility to learn from those around us.
Bless us with decisiveness when we have to move quickly.
Bless our lazy moments
    when we need to stretch out limbs for the journey.
Bless us, lead us, love us,
And bring us home, bearing the Gospel of life. Amen.

We should glory
in the cross
of our Lord Jesus Christ,
for he is our salvation,
our life and our resurrection,
through him we are saved and made free.
Amen.

Prayer before a crucifix

Lord, by this sweet and saving Sign,
Defend us from our foes and thine.

Jesu, by thy wounded feet,
    Direct our path aright;
Jesu, by thy nailed hands,
    Move ours to deeds of love;
Jesu, by thy pierced side,
    Annihilate our pride;
Jesu, by thy silence,
    Shame our complaints;
Jesu, by thy parched lips,
    Curb our cruel speech;
Jesu, by thy closing eyes,
    Look on our sin no more;
Jesu, by thy broken heart,
    Knit ours to thee.

And by this sweet and saving Sign,
Lord, draw us to our peace and thine. Amen.
                 (Richard Crawshaw – adapted)

1

Hearing: Palm Sunday

The crowds who went in front of him and those who followed were all shouting:

> Hosanna to the son of David!
> Blessed is he who comes in the name of the Lord!
> Hosanna in the highest heavens!

And when he entered Jerusalem, the whole city was in turmoil as people asked, 'Who is this?' and the crowds answered, 'This is the prophet Jesus from Nazareth in Galilee.'

(Matthew 21.9–11, NJB)

The echo effect

It was a cult movie in the 1980s. Jean-Jacques Beineix's *Diva* is film noir, underscoring surreal French humour with a sharp, swiftly moving plot, haunting camera work, and stunning music.

The story is essentially about the theft of a besotted fan's illicit recording of his diva, an opera singer who has consistently refused to sing in anything other than live performances. After a lot of excitement the fan recovers the recording and plays it to the diva in the Opéra, Paris, where it was recorded. She is overwhelmed: 'I have never heard myself sing before.'

Most of us experience a sense of discomfort when hearing a recording of our own voice. But something more is suggested by the diva's response. Singing lies at the heart of the sound of Christian worship. We are uplifted by the mass singing of popular hymns and, equally, haunted by ancient plainsong chants. The rhythmic flow of plainsong also invariably presents us with an inheritance that the Church shares with the people of Israel: the psalms.

In this chapter we shall explore how the psalms form a vital element in worship as the activity in which we seek to experience the relationship between earth and heaven. There are many ways in which the psalms are used in Christian worship, but perhaps their most obvious location is in the offices of Morning and Evening Prayer. No longer are these offices regarded as the exclusive preserve of clergy and the religious orders; many lay Christians have adopted a rule of life that includes some form of daily office.

Hearing the echo of a place

I have recently had to get used to living with a nine-second echo, as I participate in the worshipping life of St Paul's Cathedral. It means that if – when – you make a mistake or say something foolish, you have to endure the unstoppable existence of your folly for the whole duration of those nine seconds. It's as though you are hearing what you sound like for the first time, discovering a voice that is you, speaking back not as an answer, but as a sometimes terrifying revelation of what you say, and what you are like.

Just as the psalms meld together the very human and the exceptionally holy, so also there are times when the echo of our human voices can function as the more sacred voice of the building itself. Sometimes the sound of worship can exactly express the heavenly image that the wood, stone, glass and marble of St Paul's seek to portray. In these moments words and music give voice to the cherubic heads in the choir stalls as they seem to echo back, one to another: 'Holy, holy, holy.' And in the quire ceiling of the cathedral the mosaic angels that watchfully support the text and images of the *Benedicite, omnia opera*, can, with our voices, be heard to echo that same Old Testament hymn, 'O all ye works of the Lord, bless ye the Lord'.

The echo of the psalms has similarly been understood to resonate from the heart of God, whom they praise and envisaged as dwelling in glory, in the Holy of Holies in the Temple in Jerusalem: 'Lift up your hands in the sanctuary: and praise the Lord. The Lord that made heaven and earth: give thee blessing out of Sion' (Psalm 134. 2–3, BCP). The psalms absorb sensations of longing, loss, jealousy, anger, pain and vengeance into the imagination of a liturgical poetry that seeks to articulate our deepest perceptions about God and about ourselves. Their cries bounce against the immensity of God and then echo back to us a statement of the scale of our own finitude.

But as an echo inspires wonder at the scale and majesty of the building or mountainside from which it comes, so the psalms also prompt us to seek the deep presence from which the various categories of our own experiences have resonated. With the psalmist, there will be moments when we protest and hurl our praise defiantly because we hurt in grief, or we grieve in moving house, we change our jobs and experience disappointment, our marriage breaks down and anger mixes with shame and rejection. Like the release of the silent worship hidden 'beyond' the cherubic and angelic figures that decorate St Paul's, so we can find in the echo of worship some new quality that points beyond the limits of our own suffering, suggesting that in the echo God speaks.

Christian hymnody, like the psalms, is familiar with the quest to identify divine love beyond an echo of human experience:

> God is love: and he enfoldeth
>   All the world in one embrace;
> With unfailing grasp he holdeth
>   Every child of every race.
> And when human hearts are breaking
>   Under sorrow's iron rod,
> Then they find the selfsame aching
>   Deep within the heart of God.

Here we find allusion that deepens through layer upon layer of experience the power of the echo of familiar words. I remember singing this hymn on the last day I went to Sherborne Abbey before going to theological college to train for the priesthood. That day marked the end of a very happy period of my life and I felt great apprehension about the future. Whenever I have heard it since I am reminded of the experience of departure, loss and a new, slow, uncertain beginning. In this way the echo of such moments becomes personally and intimately attached to public words used by everyone in worship. We are bound to those words emotionally, just as God redemptively binds himself to us.

Sometimes, however, the psalmist also describes the loss of an echo that seems to have gone away. God is silent. To the outpouring of emotion there is no response and the worshipper laments. 'O God, wherefore art thou absent from us so long?' (Psalm 74.1, BCP) 'Hold not thy tongue, O God, keep not still silence: refrain not thyself, O God' (Psalm 83.1, BCP).

By no means is it unusual to experience in worship or prayer the sensation that there is nothing or no one there.

These are times when our words rebound emptily upon us: 'I am weary of crying; my throat is dry' (Psalm 69.3, BCP). How do we cope with this experience, especially when it seems to be more than temporary? What becomes of an undertaking to pray some form of daily office when, beyond the struggle to find the time, we lose touch with the sense of enrichment it once brought us?

Perhaps an example from childhood might help. I have always been fascinated by the fascination that young children have with story-telling. They quickly recognize the cadences and pictures that form the shape of familiar tales, and are ready to add new favourites. At a very early age they are also intrigued by the sheer mechanism of narration, often wanting to touch and feel your mouth as you speak. The stories may hold no new revelation, but their telling is a reinforcement of some deep bond, making you conspirators, united to each other in the rehearsal of a familiar circumstance.

When God seems distant, our faithfulness to the routine of worship might be encouraged by this recollection of childhood. We often expect, with adult sensitivity, a quantifiable attainment from our activity, irrespective of what the activity is. But a bedtime story does not readily admit that kind of assessment. Factors vary: novelty and familiarity, the recognized voice – and story voices – and the process of narration. At times these variables may fail to be satisfactory. But what always matters is the communication of intent: that statement of time given for the gradual and determined formation of a bond in which both of you have agreed to enter a different world, to live by imagination and not by other laws.

In this respect we might find that worship in its routine familiar form, especially the office of Morning or Evening Prayer, can also function at a variety of levels. It may or may not disclose new revelation. We may or may not feel able to get in touch with the mechanism of its ordering. The voice with which it is articulated may or may not encourage devotion. ('Who is that ecclesiastical Alf Garnett?' I once heard a bishop declare in exasperation during a sermon from a visiting preacher!) We may, like the psalmist, be jaded by the flat and echoless sound of our own voice.

In seeking to discover how we become attuned, the example of the child fascinated by the process of story-telling may offer a model for the adult. Disconnected, as child or adult, from any capacity to appreciate some greater significance (whether in the story line, or in discernment of the presence of God), we may finger with wonder the lips that tell the words. In adult terms this can mean that we continue with devotion and reverence to say the prayers we have committed ourselves to saying, for no other reason than that we understand the worth of the saying. For, as adults, we can know with our minds what our hearts long to feel, and therefore we can continue to value the exercise, even when we hear no echo.

In *A Taste for Death* the detective novelist P. D. James gives a contemporary description of this undertaking of prayer when the echo is absent, and has been for some time. The novel ends with a statement of great insight into the humility and cost of Christian discipleship today, challenging us to meet the demand of faithfulness and recognize its character in those who may be considered inconsequential by worldly standards.

The elderly sacristan whose church was the scene of the murder and whose young companion Darren has been sent away to foster parents returns to St Matthew's for the first time:

> Miss Wharton, still trembling, locked the outside door, went along the passage to the grille and gazed up

through the church to the red glow of the sanctuary
lamp. She thought . . . (God) wasn't any longer in the
church. Like Darren, he had gone away. Then she
remembered what Father Collins had once said in a
sermon when she first came to St Matthew's: 'If you find
that you no longer believe, act as if you still do. If you feel
that you can't pray, go on saying the words.' She knelt
down on the hard floor, supporting herself with her
hands grasping the iron grille and said the words with
which she always began her private prayers: 'Lord I am
not worthy that thou shouldest come under my roof, but
speak the word only and my soul shall be healed.'

When God is silent, we may be unsure that the repeating of
words will bring back the closeness that we crave. But what
else do we have except words that are the tokens of our will?
In this passage by P. D. James I feel humbled by the
strength of will that Miss Wharton invests in kneeling on
the hard floor, with some difficulty as she grasps the grille to
support herself. And, more importantly, I admire the sum-
moning of inner strength with which she picks up the
broken, desecrated threads of the practice of her faith and
speaks the familiar prayer that she hopes and tentatively
trusts will still echo in the heart of God.

Hearing the echo in creation
The advice to Miss Wharton to 'go on saying the words'
draws on the wisdom not only of St Augustine's observation
that in prayer 'our voices re-echo in Christ and his in us', but
also on St Paul's perception that 'the Spirit itself bears witness with our spirit that we are children of God' (Romans
8.16, NJB). We pray to the Father in Christ, by the power of
the Holy Spirit, even though at times the experience of this
truth feels uncertain. This perception of Christian prayer is

9

fundamental to our understanding of its relational character. Prayer is not simply my activity: it commits me to the life of all who pray, and implicates me with them in the life of God. It has something of the bonding aspect of the bedtime story experience of childhood.

The echo of prayer, however, opens up to us new boundaries of language, relationship and time. As musical but spoken compositions, the psalms resonate in the heart of God and in other directions as well. Psalm 19 suggests, for example, that in addition to the echo of human experience and longing, there is an echo throughout time:

> The heavens declare the glory of God: and the firmament sheweth his handy-work.
> One day telleth another: and one night certifieth another.
> There is neither speech nor language: but their voices are heard among them. (Psalm 19.1–3, BCP)

The notion of the sheer glory of God being itself a language that shouts from one day to the next is what motivates and shapes the pattern of daily worship in the Church. The offices of Morning and Evening Prayer, in whatever form they exist, sanctify time as they give voice in human language to the wordless acclamation of praise that the psalmist identifies in the passing of day into night and on to the return again of day.

This is a point at which the musical character of the psalms is instructive. Music is woven out of time. It is composed of quantities of measured time given particular sounds and the momentum of rhythm. Participation in the rhythm of a particular type of music can therefore express a distinctive intention. The eighth-century Celtic poet Bláthmac declares to the Virgin Mary in a poem about the crucifixion that he will mourn for Jesus: 'With you I may beat my two palms for your son.' Just as we clap together in time to indicate shared participation, so this poet seems to use that same method of ritualized rhythm to identify with the death of Jesus. Here the marking of time in the form of a beat becomes a mechanism for transcending time; making the past present, taking the present into the eternal through uniting oneself with the mystery of the Passion.

Anthony Storr also touches on this relationship between music, time and eternity in his book, *Music and the Mind*. He refers, among other composers, to Stravinsky and his 'conception of music as involved with eternity and the promotion of religious feelings of communion with God'. This is something that brings together time measured as it actually is, and the slower or swifter passing of time as we emotionally experience it.

When we think of the tremendous emotion that can be released by the singing of a hymn, both aspects of the impact of the music should be recognized. Stravinsky terms them 'ontological' (time as it actually is) and 'psychological' (time driven by emotive impulse). Anthony Storr connects these ways of understanding music by reference to movement as both a coherent unit of musical identity and an emotional or spiritual human journey through time.

In one of his sermons, Augustine makes this same connection between music and motion: 'Sing up – and keep on walking.' As we make the pilgrim journey of life, prayer is time consciously set aside in which we seek to become familiar with the rhythm of words that flow to the beat of eternity.

Sometimes the tide of overwhelming emotion will carry the tide of our prayer time; sometimes it will have to be beaten out with the slow hand-clap of endurance in a passion of willed oblation. But whatever the circumstance, it connects, in its echo, with the heartbeat of divine, triunal life.

The glory of God declared in the heavens is the way in which we measure our time, in the rising and setting of the sun and the passing of the seasons of the year. Here the divine ordering of the rhythm of the universe calls us to keep pace with its beat by our releasing the work of prayer and sanctification.

The disconnectedness of our Western society from this primal rhythm of days and seasons is in marked contrast to so much of the scriptural ordering of prayer. We do not generally think of time in terms of sabbaths and jubilees. But these categories lie not far beneath the surface in Christian tradition that understands the significance of facing east. As William Temple observed: 'Only if God is revealed in the rising of the sun in the sky can he be revealed in the rising of a son of man from the dead.'

Anyone who has watched the sun rise or set knows what a powerful moment it is when the huge smouldering disc slips below the horizon. This display of changing light, colour and heat, says Psalm 104, is like the design of a costume for the appearance of God on the stage of creation in order to reveal God's glory:

> Praise the Lord, O my soul: O Lord my God, thou art
> become exeeding glorious; thou art clothed with majesty
> and honour.
> Thou deckest thyself with light as it were with a
> garment: and spreadest out the heavens like a curtain.
>
> (104.1–2, BCP)

Our fascination with this curtain of light and darkness, snow, mist, wind and rain that we experience was explored in a hugely popular installation in the Tate Modern in 2003. 'The Weather Project' by Olafur Eliasson illustrated a subject matter close to the English heart, as Samuel Johnson observed: 'When two Englishmen meet, their first talk is of the weather; they are in haste to tell each other what each must already know, that it is hot or cold, bright or cloudy.'

The guide to Eliasson's installation describes 'The Weather Project':

> Through the day, the mist accumulates into faint cloud-like formations, before dissipating across the space.
> A glance overhead, to see where the mist might escape, reveals that the ceiling of the Turbine Hall has disappeared, replaced by a huge mirror reflecting the space below. At the far end of the hall is a giant semi-circular form . . . (which) repeated in the mirror produces a sphere of dazzling radiance linking the real space with the reflection.

The mirror ceiling had the effect of committing anyone who entered the Turbine Hall to participate in the installation in a variety of ways.

On my first visit to 'The Weather Project', with older friends, we discussed its artistic merits in a rather grown-up, Radio 4-like way. But I soon returned, to do what other people were doing: lie on the floor and simply look up at the extraordinary configurations of humanity reflected above. There we caught, as it were, a visual echo of ourselves in what might have represented the 'curtain' of glory with which God is 'clothed'. What impressed me was the fact that in the reflection I could locate myself, but only in relation to other people. It was not my reflection I was looking at, but ours. With delight and fascination I was effortlessly released from isolation, but without loss of individuality. There was no choice but to belong to the reflection.

Those around me formed a vital part of the echo of myself, as I did of them, and many people were very engaged in being themselves in ways that intrigued and amused us all, with children running in and out of clumps of adults who themselves became uninhibited in child-like play. One group arrived and began a kind of performance, spelling out in human bodies the word 'HELLO' and ending their display with 'BYE!', which drew a round of applause. It was not very British. But it was very human and very close to a scriptural grasp of delight in the echo between God and the work of creation that is brilliantly identified with the Old Testament figure of Wisdom, a fresh and luminous spirit, unfettered by the cranking machinery of laboured study:

> When he traced the foundations of the earth,
> I was beside the master craftsman,
> delighting him day after day,
> ever at play in his presence,
> at play everywhere on his earth,
> delighting in the human race.
>
> (Proverbs 8.29–31, NJB)

Mesmerized by the vast orb and the visual echo of the mirror ceiling, we were able to achieve the moment of perception that Eliasson described as 'seeing yourselves sensing'. I don't know whether Eliasson has any Christian faith, but the experience that he facilitated at Tate Modern certainly seemed to me to be profoundly expressive of the echo effect of worship, demonstrated by the psalms and linked with the rising and setting of the sun in the daily offices of Morning and Evening Prayer as the sanctification of time.

Hearing the echo in time

One of the oldest Christian hymns is the *Phos Hilarion* ('O gladsome light'), an evening celebratory statement of praise, shot through with a sense of utter joy at the sight of the setting sun. Our derivation of the word 'hilarity' from the Greek title of this hymn indicates how far notions of rejoicing have changed. 'Gladsome' may now be too formal a word to convey the scope of joy intended, while 'hilarity' veers towards cheap jokes and fairgrounds. The 'feel-good factor' may perhaps be a closer translation in contemporary idiom, if that phrase can be detached from self-centred shopping and consumerism and located instead in shared experience, such as a street party, wedding or New Year celebration.

The rhythm of prayer that takes its beat from the workings of creation finds a harmony in which all human striving, anguish and loss are wound into the kaleidoscopic glory of God's redemptive revelation. Without in any sense diminishing the reality of suffering, hope is nonetheless kindled by the cadences of this harmony, and with that hope comes something 'gladsome'. In this rhythm, pounding universally through hymns and psalms in soaring plainsong, isolated simplicity and myriad languages, time becomes praise. This praise is the liberation of time from its identity as the keeper of our mortality and the herald of death. Praise, in which we regard time as a source of indescribable joy, contrasts sharply with the 'time is money' mortgaging of our lives to the faceless, global, competitive and economic forces that determine so much of our life as work.

Nowhere are those forces more obviously present than in the City of London. As an international centre for banking, insurance and law, the City understands all too well the financial and social value of time. Here hourly rates can be measured in figures greater than the amount some people earn in a week or in a year. Stress, burnout, dysfunctional relationships, loss of identity and the appetite for life, all the world-weariness described by the French as *ennui*, these things were long ago recognized by T. S. Eliot as elements of life in the City. Eliot described it as a wasteland, the title of

his 1922 collection of poems, written on the brink of his conversion to Christianity. In 'The Burial of the Dead', the first
poem from that collection, entitled *The Wasteland*, he
writes:

> Unreal City,
> Under the brown fog of a winter dawn,
> A crown flowed over London Bridge, so many,
> I had not thought death had undone so many.
> Sighs, short and infrequent, were exhaled,
> And each man fixed his eyes before his feet.
> Flowed up the hill and down King William Street,
> To where Saint Mary Woolnoth kept the hours
> With a dead sound on the final stroke of nine.

Eliot sees time as the symbol of death and finality for this
crowd whose working day is imprisoned within its boundaries. For the City workforce, time may have ceased to be a
gift in which to discover the rhythm of praise that sanctifies
and irradiates life. Instead it becomes the measurement by
which you are paid in a currency that is not eternal.

In this wasteland, however, the City churches stand as
places where it is possible to be refreshed by time regained.
Here time is not money; it resonates with the echo of the
eternal. The City churches hold within them what Eliot calls
'inexplicable splendours', architectural statements of something that is 'beyond understanding'. These are boundaries
of space from which the echo of our human aspirations for
peace, for a break, for dignity, for love, for forgiveness, might
be heard. These are places where time is transcended by the
echo from our praise, where the rhythm of heaven might be
detected.

When we perceive by our senses the atmosphere and
significance of a building, perhaps we can also begin to

understand the events of Palm Sunday and the echo of divine presence within them. In the Gospels of Matthew and Luke the entry into Jerusalem is heralded by crowds of singing people. The cleansing of the Temple draws our attention to a building in which the redemptive action of God will be represented, and Matthew's Gospel underlines the connection between body and building with reference to healing miracles.

Here the themes that we have been exploring converge in the actions of Jesus. The praise of psalmody, expressed within the body as in a building, now finds an echo in the visible activity of God who is made manifest in Jesus. Palm Sunday is a day of resonance, of echoes, and it is to this day that we turn our attention.

Hearing the Palm Sunday echo
Matthew's description of the entry into Jerusalem and the cleansing of the Temple is far more detailed than that of the other evangelists. The whole of Jerusalem is in a state of great turbulence. In the Temple three things seem to take place at the same time: Jesus deals with the traders, he cures the blind and the lame, and the children continue their chanting while the chief priests begin to protest. One might wonder whether this is a 'We don't like noisy children in church' complaint, or whether it is driven by a theological distaste for what the children are saying. That uncertainty is by no means unfamiliar to many parents and parish priests today! But Jesus is unmoved by the objections. On the first Palm Sunday in Jerusalem, however, the complaint was definitely official, and Luke describes it in these terms: "'Master, reprove your disciples." But Jesus answered, "I tell you, if these keep silent, the stones will cry out'" (Luke 19.39–40, NJB).

This is the second time that Jesus has caused turmoil in Jerusalem, according to Matthew. The first was when the

Magi came in search of a new king, and here, again, it was children that bore the brunt of adult fear in the massacre that ensued. As Jesus arrives to confront his death, the disturbance deepens into a turmoil that has a darker echo. Matthew underscores the significance of the entry into Jerusalem by describing it as something seismic. Buildings, and the very earth itself, echo with the impact of this turmoil. It is a moment of – literally – ground-breaking significance, shaking the buildings and the human city and again, later in Matthew's account, shaking the earth and splitting the rocks when Jesus dies on Good Friday.

What does the sound of this seismic moment hit in order to echo back to us through time? Where is the endpoint of death? Against what part of life expectancy do we pin the death of a person we loved and say, 'I always knew that could happen?' In *Paradise Lost*, John Milton accurately describes that reality and endpoint as the moment of the Fall, the first bite of the apple, when discord broke upon the world and all creation registered the event:

> Earth felt the wound, and Nature from her seat,
> Sighing through all her works, gave signs of woe
> That all was lost.

Matthew recognizes that Jerusalem is in turmoil – seismically – because a song is being sung to greet Jesus Christ, the new Adam and high priest who alone can heal the wound that was inflicted by the disobedience of the first Adam. That wound is death. And the song that is being sung comes from Psalm 118: 'Blessed is he who is coming in the name of the Lord! Hosanna in the highest' (118.26, NJB).

The image and language of this psalm belong to the Temple and the ritual of the Day of Atonement. The word 'Hosanna' means 'Save us' and it is addressed to the 'one who

18

comes in the name of the Lord'. The Old Testament scholar, Margaret Barker, has written a great deal that illuminates for us the power and endurance of the images of Temple worship. They provided the language and symbolism used in the earliest Christian churches to understand the person and work of Jesus. They almost certainly shaped the religious culture from which Jesus drew and therefore how he understood his vocation.

In *The Great High Priest* Margaret Barker makes the point that in Hebrew the phrase 'in the name' and 'with the name' is identical. Themes of kingship and priesthood are interwoven in the liturgy of the Temple, but it seems certain that the royal, priestly figure who ministered there wore a band around the turban on his head on which was written the name of the LORD, the name of God.

It is a royal and priestly figure that the psalmist acclaims, and as the people on the streets of Jerusalem sing their song to acclaim the entry of Jesus, what they are saying, in modern idiom, is that Jesus 'has the name of God written all over him'. So Matthew is saying that a seismic echo from the earth is recognition that Jesus is the eternal priest who alone can heal the world's wounds because his history touches the endpoint of creation in the 'Let there be' beginning of Genesis. And we might reflect that this seismic echo is in response to a song from Psalm 118.

We began this chapter with the comment from the diva in Jean-Jacques Beineix's film: 'I have never heard myself sing before.' How might this describe our participation in public worship and personal prayer? What echoes resonate within our hearts when we pray? How will our voices implicate us in the liturgy of Holy Week, beginning with Palm Sunday? The answers lie, I think, in attempts to silence the song we are called to sing.

Luke (19.40) records that the Pharisees tell Jesus to

reprove those who were singing the dangerous words, from Psalm 118.26, of priestly recognition and welcome: 'Blessed is he who is coming as King *with* the name of the Lord.' Jesus replies: 'I tell you, if these keep silence, the stones will cry out.' What is interesting is the relationship between the stones and Jesus. Shortly after this exchange with the Pharisees, Jesus quotes back to them some other words from Psalm 118.22: 'the stone which the builders rejected has become the cornerstone', clearly applying those words to himself.

Since Jesus understands the significance of applying the image of the cornerstone from Psalm 118 to himself, then as a kind of parable we can think of the stones as able to sing. And then we might say that the Pharisees had been active throughout the ministry of Jesus in wanting to silence the echo of psalmody within those stones that would otherwise have sung a song in recognition of the divine presence and work of redemption.

The Pharisees steal the echo from them and gave in exchange stony silence. But on Palm Sunday, the people of Jerusalem gave back to the Temple stones the song of recognition. Like us, the crowds that chant hosannas give to the building an echo that returns more than it received. In the echo from the stones, Jesus is recognized as the one who comes to fulfil the sacrifices the Temple had housed in time, but that he will offer in time and eternity.

In this way, Palm Sunday speaks to us about more than simply hearing the chants of that particular day. This day speaks about cosmic audibility. This is the day on which the echo between earth and heaven, between time and eternity, is heard with the kind of clarity that Milton described as attending the moment of the Fall.

That is why Matthew describes it as a seismic day. And that is also why the Pharisees, like Herod three decades earlier, are afraid; because there is something, someone here who disturbs their world by the introduction of a power greater than anything they can control.

For further reflection ...

Prayer and pressure

The Pharisees were by no means an unsophisticated, uncivilized or unintelligent group. They would be at home in an office, school or university and their qualities would deserve recognition. But their reasonableness also facilitates death.

Prayer, like language that is subversive, can be silenced for a variety of ostensibly good reasons. 'It is better for one man to die for the people,' declared Caiaphas the high priest when, in John's account, the decision was taken to plot the death – and therefore silence – of Jesus.

- Do you have an adequate and realistic pattern (time, place, forms) of prayer?
- What are the pressures that silence the voice of your daily prayer? How can they be resisted?
- Have you ever asked for guidance and help with sustaining this part of your Christian life?

Prayer and power

The controlling power of the Pharisees silenced the echo of the stones. But from elsewhere God inspired a language and music that those in power could not control.

So it is in our society. Christians themselves may find it disconcerting to hear the need for justice, human dignity, access to medicine and education, a decent home, food and a job, articulated by those who claim no Christian faith and may even be critical of it. Such voices may belong to local politicians, other faith groups, schools, medical or community centres, neighbouring churches. A survey of the national and local papers on any day is likely to provide evidence of this.

- Where are these voices to be found in your community and neighbourhood?
- What they are saying? Do their statements resonate with the demands of the kingdom of heaven?
- How would you register your refusal to be silenced?
- At what point would you write a letter or send an e-mail of protest?
  (This is still one of the most powerful weapons for an organization like Amnesty International.)

Prayer and the demons

The uncomfortable words of the psalms can expose our evasion of the things we fear. For example, the psalms express passion, anger, grief and resentment. Worship that does not lay the demons of these emotions before God cannot make the oblation of all that we are.

The psalms strip from us layers of defence; they provoke our tears and illuminate our weaknesses. If we do not recognize that fault-lines can be ours, we shall never learn to forgive the weaknesses of others, or love the strength with which they bear them.

In the tentative enterprise of prayer we claim the freedom to be ourselves, while at the same time fingering the mystery of words that are known to have revealed seismic power. These are words that we offer because we know that there is echo within them, even when we do not hear it ourselves.

- In what language do you express to God the extremities of your emotional life?
- How do you cope when God seems silent and prayer seems pointless?

- Where might you find the prayer support of other Christians to uphold you?
- What forms of prayer, perhaps best known by heart, do you use to collect and offer before God your tears and guilt?

For a group . . .

1. Scripture reading

1 Samuel 3.1–4.1: The call of Samuel

Luke 4.16–30: Jesus echoes the words of Isaiah

These readings raise questions about the way in which we hear the word and call of God, and the confusing circumstances in which it might occur. We also recognize that admiration is not to be sought at the cost of authenticity.

2. Music and film

Members of the group bring a recording of a very short piece of music and explain how it speaks to them about the echo of the presence of God.

This is also an opportunity to watch the short sequence from the video *Diva* that is mentioned at the beginning of this section. Alternatively, a sequence from Roman Polanski's film *The Pianist* could be shown (available on DVD). Towards the end of the film, the pianist Wladyslaw Szpilman, hiding in a bombed-out house in Warsaw, is discovered by a Nazi officer and asked to play the piano. Szpilman is depicted with agonized, Christ-like features, pouring out a cry for redemption from the heart of human suffering and destruction.

3. The echo effect

Questions for discussion:

- How does the sound of your worship in church provide the inspiration to hear the 'echo effect', and gain a sense of

worship on earth being in tune with worship in heaven?
- Prayer grows and deepens through the rhythm of its practice in daily life; what shared rhythms of prayer do you have? Is the saying of the daily office a part of this?
- Liturgy is designed to sanctify time: does your marking of the seasons adequately identify this intention?
- What place is there for stillness in your worship? How do you prepare for its distractions and grow into familiarity with silence as a statement of the presence of God?
- What aspect of the Palm Sunday liturgy will create the biggest impact? How will it convey the message you wish to communicate?

Reflection

Behind each face and voice lies the silence of the heart.
This silence is as old as the universe.
It holds within it a time
before vegetation clothed the earth
or animal walked or sound echoed.
This silence waits quietly under thoughts,
beneath actions, relationships,
behind days, nights and names.
No one owns this silence.
No one can force it out into the light.
Yet it is in this sanctuary
that experience is sifted and transfigured.
It is where our vanished days secretly gather.
This silence is the home
of memory and identity.
It houses the spirit
which coheres,
articulates
and shapes
each human life.

(John O'Donohue)

2

Taste: Maundy Thursday

'The Master says this to you: Where is the room for me to eat the Passover with my disciples?' The man will show you a large upper room furnished with couches. Make the preparations there.

(Luke 22.11–12, NJB)

Serious about food

I was a student in Oxford for two years. For most of that time I was cheerfully broke and in search of recreation that was moral, stimulating and free. I found it in the covered market. It was food.

Food, with its primary stimulation of the sense of taste, in fact draws upon all the senses for the appreciation of its varied qualities. Surveying the food stalls of the covered market relieved the tedium of study with a burst of sensual enchantment. The smell of fresh fish, the texture of pheasant plumage, the muted colours of autumn apples, yellow plums and waxen pomegranates, and the sound of grinding coffee beans conspired to give my taste buds the impression that I had been treated to a fabulous meal. In reality, I might only have bought and eaten a Mars bar.

There is no doubt that at a very basic level of our emotional life, food is a source of comfort. But how seriously do we take our food? It is surely an irony that at the same time as we consume more hours of television devoted to cookery and happily buy the ever-greater range of glossy books they produce, we actually spend less and less time in preparing the food we eat. I could probably live without many things I currently take for granted, but easily persuade myself that the local supermarket's range of oven-ready meals is unlikely to be one of them. And beyond the question of pre-prepared food, our more serious concerns about the unhealthy content of fast food, snacks and drinks ought surely to take into account the dysfunctional aspects of our life that make eating in excess and badly so popular and inevitable.

My recollection of the covered market in Oxford is amply reinforced by Caravaggio's painting, 'The Supper at Emmaus'. That painting evokes the Christian emphasis on the essential nature of the Church as expressed in the communal experience of a meal. The visual impact of the painting suggests that the sense of taste is a pointer to the profound significance of food and is very important to us. However, contemporary life may not encourage us to treat with much seriousness our food or the meal that is the theatre in which its qualities are exhibited.

One of the most distinctive aspects of the alternative lifestyle of a religious community is the way that meals are taken. In a large monastery one might well discover that the refectory in which one eats appears to have an atmosphere not very different from that of the conventual church. The table of the Eucharist and the meal table are housed with dignity and approached with similar decorum. Nor is conversation necessarily the way in which community life is deepened by eating together; silence waiting upon each other, and the shared sensations of taste in what is provided suggest a unity that is generally unfamiliar to us in secular life.

Outside the measured life of the cloister, however, we probably no longer expect to eat together regularly at a table; it's fine to munch on the street, the bus or the train. The structure of our day is more varied; meal times are when you are hungry or when you are free. They are often unscheduled and therefore require there to be little or no preparation. And for city dwellers, a take-away cappuccino is virtually a morning fashion accessory. We live with the exceptional privilege of food in great abundance and prepared for us. Some shops will even sell ready-peeled oranges, enticing us into oblivion towards the processes of growth, harvest, marketing and preparation in which unpalatable residues of unjust trading and human exploitation lurk with no easy detection.

In this chapter we enquire into how the sense of taste functions in the context of the Christian life and our contemporary experience. Jesus leaves his disciples with a meal as the means by which they remember him. Those who thereafter participate in that meal identify themselves as connected to him. The connection is physical; you can taste it. But it is also moral: a statement about embodiment that draws together every aspect of our lives, just as our appreciation of food draws a response from all our senses. How does this eating habit, the Eucharist, inform our sense of the presence of God which is beyond sensation? How does it shape the way we order our responsibilities and relationships?

Returning to the point about food as a source of comfort, we might do well to begin our enquiry with the most fundamental and natural of all foods: mother's milk. And in this instance, the obvious example to begin with is that of the Virgin Mary.

Taste and compassion

In a fascinating book (*Empress and Handmaid*) about the significance of devotion to Mary, Sarah Boss identifies a link between the image of Mary the nursing mother and the Eucharist. In the parish church of St Mary, Great Canfield, in Essex, an early-thirteenth-century wall painting was discovered last century above the high altar. The painting shows Jesus, depicted as a miniature adult seated on his mother's lap. It is evident that there are unusual time frames operative here. Mary is the earthly mother and extends her breast to Jesus in a way that appears to be biologically improbable, but makes sense if understood as symbol. But she is also crowned and seated on a throne as a statement of risen life in the presence of God. This is an affirmation that the human experience of being fed has some kind of resonance with the experience of heaven.

Later medieval paintings that depict Mary exposing her breast to feed the Christ child often have other details within them that help us to read the interpretation of the gesture that would have made sense to Christians of the fifteenth century, but not to us. Carol Walker Bynum has pointed out in her book *Holy Feast and Holy Fast* that the connection between blood and milk was a familiar one in medieval devotion: 'What writers of the high Middle Ages wished to say about Christ the saviour who feeds the individual soul with his own blood was precisely and concisely said in the image of the nursing mother whose milk *is* her blood, offered to the child.'

An obvious symbol that states this in a different way is that of the pelican. Frequently applied to the Eucharist, the image of the bird that pecks its own breast so that it bleeds in order to feed its young is a statement about the self-offering of Jesus on the cross. Medieval devotion slips with ease between images that belong to one gender or another, without implying any doubt about the historical identity of the person in question. So it is that the Lady Julian of Norwich can write in her *Revelations of Divine Love*: 'The human mother may put her child tenderly to her breast, but our tender Mother Jesus simply leads us into his blessed breast through his open side.'

The meal of the Eucharist and what we taste within it is explored in a variety of images that make an identification between the breast of Jesus, pierced with the lance on the cross, and that of Mary as the source of nurture, comfort and compassion for the Christ child. In the National Gallery in London there is a fifteenth-century painting of the 'Virgin and Child' by Robert Campin. Mary rests her arm on a cupboard on which stands a chalice. The detail is almost certainly a modification made in the nineteenth century, but the fact that it could be located there at all makes explicit an understanding, almost certainly known to the artist, of the connection between the blood of the Eucharist and the mother's milk.

Carol Walker Bynum has sought to push the imagery of this painting further. Campin's picture locates Mary in front of a fire screen, beyond which we can just see the top of the flames. Possibly prompted by this element in the painting, Bynum alludes to Jesus as akin to fresh bread from an oven. The allusion is not of her own invention: it obviously draws on the imagery of the eucharistic bread and was originally stated in a hugely popular medieval work of devotion, *Meditations on the Life of Christ*, the authorship of which was attributed to St Bonaventure. Writing about the annunciation, the author of the *Meditations* declares that the Feast of the Annunciation is the day on which 'the living bread that animates the world has begun to be baked in the oven of the virginal womb'.

We might snigger coyly about 'a bun in the oven'. But for

the medieval Christian, the beautiful aroma and the expectation of the taste of fresh bread were statements about the sanctification of all life, including the purposes of human sexuality, in the incarnation. Here we are reminded of a generation that met the compassionate God who sustained their life through the providence of the harvest and the work of human hands. The immediacy of this providence is rather more difficult for us to sense today through the invisible food chain that ends in our local supermarket.

Another painting from the fifteenth century, by Joos van Cleve, shows Mary against a darkening sky looking sombrely into the distance as the Christ child sleeps at the breast from which he has been feeding. In the book open on her lap, Mary traces with a finger the prophecy of the scriptures about her son, who holds an apple, the symbol of the Fall. In front of both mother and child a sharp knife has opened an aptly named passion fruit, a pomegranate has been sliced in two revealing its seeds that are a symbol of resurrection, while a bowl of fruit in front of Mary stands as a general expression of charity. The red cloth spread over Mary's lap subtly extends the same colour of blood into the wine in the covered beaker that stands next to the grapes, its glass translucently connecting wine and the meal cloth on the nursing mother's knee.

In the symbolism that is attached to these fruits, the Church has invariably drawn on older traditions and applied them to its own story of love, union and redemption. This symbolism evokes the compassion of God, functioning at the most basic level of a parent feeding its child. The demonstration of this at its most intense in the Old Testament is in the experience of the exodus and the 40-year-long pilgrimage to the promised land: 'I am the Lord thy God, who brought thee out of the land of Egypt: open thy mouth wide and I will fill it' (Psalm 81.10, BCP).

Here the compassion of God bears with the people whose sense of taste tempts them back to the comforts of Egypt: 'If only we had died by the hand of the Lord in the land of Egypt, when we sat by the fleshpots and ate our fill of bread.' To this God responds, 'At twilight you shall eat meat, and in the morning you shall have your fill of bread; then you will know that I am the Lord your God' (Exodus 16.3, 12, NRSV).

The meal that forms this manifestation of the compassion of God for the people of Israel is also a marriage banquet. It is in the wilderness that their betrothal is sealed, as the prophets Jeremiah and Hosea both suggest: 'Thus says the Lord, "I remember the devotion of your youth, your love as a bride, how you followed me in the wilderness."' (Jeremiah 2.2, NRSV). It is in the wilderness that Hosea sees the re-kindling of the marital bond between the Lord and Israel: 'I will now allure her, and bring her into the wilderness, and speak tenderly to her. From there I will give her her vine-yards' (Hosea 2.14–15, NRSV). The use of the vine as an allusion to marriage is not unfamiliar in the Old Testament: 'Thy wife shall be as the fruitful vine upon the walls of thy house' (Psalm 128.3, BCP). Similarly, in the New Testament it is the produce of the vine that Jesus supplies at the marriage at Cana in Galilee.

In the images of Mary and the Christ child, the presence of fruit indicates not only allusion to food as an allegory of compassion; it can also suggest the modelling of an Old Testament theme that is brought to fulfilment in the birth of Christ. The theme is that of marriage, frequently symbol-ized by the quince, a fruit that often features in paintings of the infant Jesus, but also by the wedding ring that Mary is sometimes depicted as wearing. In an older iconography the clasp by the infant Jesus of Mary's chin is a gesture that, Leo Steinbern maintains, in *The Sexuality of Christ in*

Renaissance Art and Modern Oblivion, the ancient, medieval and renaissance world would instantly have recognized as overtly amorous. Here, Mary is the symbol of the chosen people of God and the faithful bride. By an extraordinary shift of identity, her son then becomes the embodiment of the God who is her spouse.

'Taste and the art of love' could be the sub-title of a book that has had greater influence on our imaginative understanding and iconography than we sometimes recognize. The book is the Song of Songs, a text frequently plundered for Marian imagery and the reference point for many of the fruits and spices that feature in artists' decoration of pictures of Mary and the Christ child. The sense of taste is used to describe the union of love that this book so lyrically annunciates: 'As an apple tree among the trees of the wood, so is my love among young men . . . his fruit is sweet to my taste. He has taken me to his cellar [an allusion to the marriage banqueting hall] and his banner over me is love' (Song of Songs 2.3, NJB).

Taste as an expression of compassion blends here into taste as a symbol of desire and union. Characteristically, this sense, drawing on the involvement of the other four, reminds us of our identity as embodied persons, and the love that taste evokes is expressly related to bodily love and intimate relationship. This is an area of human experience that Christians can find difficult to integrate into the discourse and symbolism by which we articulate our faith. This sense provides us with an awareness of desire, temptation and indulgence that is destructive. But the allegory of taste can also function at its best in Christian discourse as a statement that all our identity as embodied persons, including all that is good in erotic love, is consumed by God in Christ.

Brief quotations from two very different books can perhaps illustrate this point. From Joanne Harris's *Chocolat,*

the stirring of desire in the midst of Lenten renunciation for
chocolate from a new and alluring shop produces temptation
in the mind of the parish priest: 'I catch a movement from
within me. *Try me. Test me. Taste me.*' This echoes St Augustine who writes in his *Confessions* of his desire for God: 'I
tasted you, and now hunger and thirst for you: you touched
me, and I have burned for your peace.' Taste is the sensation
of desire and relationship. How does the Eucharist shape the
way we relate to what is around us?

Taste and desire

> Come ye hither All, whose taste
>   Is your waste;
> Save your cost, and mend your fare.
> God is here prepar'd and drest,
>   And the feast,
> God, in whom all dainties are.
>
> Come ye hither All, whom wine
>   Doth define,
> Naming you not to your good:
> Weep what ye have drunk amisse,
>   And drink this,
> Which before ye drink is bloud.
>
> Come ye hither All, whom pain
>   Doth arraigne,
> Bringing all your sinnes to sight:
> Taste and fear not: God is here
>   In this cheer,
> And on sinne doth cast the fright.

This quotation from 'The Invitation' by George Herbert uses the meal as an allegory for the transformation of our human desires and experience. In contrast to our culture of waste, God provides the meal that satisfies every desire with 'all dainties'. Wine is presented not as last night's cause for this morning's hangover ('not to your good'), but as that blood that in communion reveals our true identity by 'bringing all your sinnes to sight' and banishing them ('on sinne doth cast the fright'). This is the meal in which our nature and relationship are revealed. We are heirs of the kingdom of heaven, and bound to each other even on earth by participation in the meal that assures our incorporation into the body of Christ, 'the blessed company of all faithful people', in the words of the Eucharist with which Herbert would have been familiar.

The 'taste and waste' experience that Herbert refers to is an interesting statement about a dysfunctional eating habit. In the other verses of the poem he extends the theme to include the pursuits of indulgence in which 'joy doth destroy' and 'love is your dove'; that is to say, it eludes our grasp. Translating these themes into a contemporary setting, we can identify how the sense of taste and its exercise in a meal continues to reveal areas in which our lives express damaging and dislocated relationships.

In the first area, the damage is to a certain extent self-inflicted through bad eating habits that are the consequence of the easy satisfaction of our desire through the abundance of the food that we who belong to the privileged world have so easily available to us. But the damage is greater than this. It is damage to the earth and to those who inhabit its least affluent, most vulnerable and exploited areas.

In many supermarkets there is a section that sells organic food. It is often more expensive and limited in range, and it is probably not very clear what organic actually means. There is no claim that it is going to taste different, but the principles that determine what food can legitimately be called organic raise questions about our treatment of the environment in the production of food that is not organic, grown more cheaply and no doubt for greater profit. The basic principle is that organic food avoids the use of chemicals in its production.

More detailed definition of organic farming includes the following considerations:

- Working with natural systems rather than seeking to dominate them.
- The encouragement of biological cycles involving micro-organisms, soil, flora and fauna, plants and animals.
- The maintenance of valuable existing landscape features and adequate habitats for the existence of wildlife, with particular reference to endangered species.
- The prevention of pollution.
- Consideration for the wider social and ecological impact of the farming system.

For most of us who live in an urban environment, farming is a remote and unfamiliar industry. We are well served by our farmers, and can easily take for granted the invaluable management that they undertake of those vast tracks of open space that provide a contrast with the city. However, we ought also to enquire whether our demand for food that is plentiful and inexpensive, and the markets in which farmers have to compete in order to supply it, does not also commit them to farming practices that cannot embrace the organic principles outlined above. Here, in the sense of laying waste the land from which we extract our food, we might perceive a modern sense in which our taste is our waste and the cost is our dislocation from the worth and refreshment of the rhythm of natural systems and biological cycles.

But it is not only the waste of the earth and the damage of our exploitative relationship to it that we should be aware of. There is a second area of damage: that of human relationships in the exploitation of the less powerful in the processes of how we trade. The Old Testament prophets are fulsome in their denunciation of those who flout the law that requires fair dealing in trade. 'You shall not cheat in measuring length, weight, or quantity. You shall have honest balances, honest weights' is the requirement of the law (Leviticus 19.35, NRSV). But Amos uncovers unjust processes by which food is supplied when trade is impatiently resumed after the interruption of religious observances:

> Hear this, you that trample on the needy, and bring to ruin the poor of the land, saying, 'When will the new moon be over so that we may sell grain; and the sabbath, so that we may offer wheat for sale? We will make the ephah small and the shekel great, and practice deceit with false balances.' (Amos 8.4–5, NRSV)

The false balances of today's world are those of power, located in the international marketplace and manifested as the producer's inability to access trade systems that ensure profits for traders but instability and debt for labourers and farmers. The most obvious example of this is in the production of coffee, a stylish commodity for city workers and the livelihood of some of the poorest people in the world. How does the balance between them sit?

A report from the Fairtrade Foundation, entitled 'Spilling the Beans', outlines some of the issues on both sides. Coffee is one of the most valuable commodities on the world market, second only after oil. But it is produced mostly in the world's poorest countries; for example, it accounts for 54 per cent of Ethiopia's foreign exchange earnings. The difficulty for coffee producers is that the price they are paid for their coffee cannot be guaranteed, so that when it fell dramatically in 2001 national economies were seriously destabilized. 'By reconnecting consumers with producers (Fairtrade) ensures that farmers get a fair price for their crops and the chance of a sustainable future.'

But coffee is not the only produce to be fairly traded with significantly beneficial effects for those who farm in developing countries. The Fairtrade Foundation website outlines the results of a survey among banana farmers and workers in the Dominican Republic. The benefits were identified in the following ways:

- Regular income: Alfredo can now provide regular food for his three children.
- Cleaner environment: Fairtrade policies have insisted on proper disposal of plastic bags used for protecting the banana crop.
- Affordable housing: Having always lived in substandard accommodation, Gregorio can now say with dignity: 'We are building something that is ours.'
- Water supplies: A pump for the local well and connection with disused pipes provides running water in the village. Water no longer has to be brought in tanks or bottles.
- School and sport: Fairtrade farmers have been able to supply uniforms and equipment.

Coffee and bananas are among the most accessible food-stuffs available to us today in the busy routine of working life. The comforting taste of each carries with it an association of relationships that we might discover to be dysfunctional. No small part of the damaging nature of those relationships is the fact that they seem so distant and unreal. There seems to be no communion between me and the individuals and communities who produce my coffee or grow my bananas. I probably have little idea of the kind of life they live or the fragility of the national economy in which my supermarket chain may have greater power than any political leader that those people may elect.

The prophet Hosea understood that dislocated relationships in trade can be symbolically represented by similar damage in the more intimate relationships of love and desire. Hosea saw the wilderness as the location of betrothal and marriage between God and Israel, his bride. By contrast, the affluence of the promised land seduces this people. Here is found the trader 'in whose hands are false balances' (Hosea 12.7, NRSV). The consequences of this infect the transactions by which the meal table is supplied; here again, taste is waste in unjustly bartered relationships. The message of symbolic prophecy against this betrayal is played out by Hosea in the extraordinary instruction he receives from God concerning the most intimate details of his life: 'Go, take for yourself a wife of whoredom . . . for the land commits great whoredom by forsaking the Lord' (Hosea 1.2, NRSV).

This connection between the degrading of intimate human relationships and the degrading of the trade by which we organize how and what we eat is neatly drawn in a film made up of a series of cameos, one of which has achieved particular notoriety. *When Harry Met Sally* presents us with two young people who meet at university and spend the next 20 years or so exploring whether or not it is possible to be just good friends.

The famous scene is set in a fast-food diner as the location for a conversation about sex. Harry (Billy Crystal) has a depersonalized view of sex that enables him to gratify his desires with no interest in emotional entanglement, believing that the women he sleeps with enjoy his attentions. Sally (Meg Ryan) believes that the women are smarter, know how to deal with the male ego, and have deluded him. At the fast-food meal table she volubly demonstrates how this deception works. The scene is brilliantly acted and ends with the best line of the whole film: an amazed older woman at the next table says to the waiter, 'I'll have what she's having.'

This film presents us with an image of serious dislocation in taste. Both food and relationships are represented by something that is tragically less than it can be, with the consequence that neither offers an authenticity of experience, as Sally's obsession with the layout of her food (but not its quality) and Harry's notches on the bedpost indicate. This is the arena of disconnected relationships in which the Eucharist is experienced as a source of healing and refreshment. The liturgy presents us with a drama that feeds, unites and satisfies desire, drawing on the common taste of a food that is universally beneficial to all in the constructing of enriching and eternal relationships.

Communion is the consequence of our participation at the meal table of the altar, uniting us with the body of Christ in the food we eat and as the people we are. It is with this perception that George Herbert ends 'The Invitation', the revelation of the all of the fullness of God indicating where the all of the human race should also meet:

> Lord I have invited all,
> And I shall
> Still invite, still call to thee:
> For it seems but just and right
> In my sight,
> Where is All, there All should be.

Taste and healing

The invitation to the Eucharist inevitably brings together those whose lives are damaged in some way, such is the nature of our humanity. But how might we understand this meal as healing that damage, and what expression of healing for the earth does it convey?

If we look at the texts of what Jesus says at the Last Supper, we see that he clearly refers to the cup of wine shared in the meal as the sign of blood that seals a covenant. Matthew records it as a covenant 'for the forgiveness of sins'; Luke states that it is a 'new covenant' (Matthew 26.28; Luke 22.20, NRSV). How does this wine that is blood heal? How does it effect the forgiveness of sins?

Margaret Barker's book, *The Great High Priest*, is once again a stimulating guide to the ways in which the Old Testament shaped the Church's understanding of who Jesus was and the significance of what he did. Of particular interest to us is the image of the damage to the earth that is a consequence to the pollution of the covenant by human sin: 'The earth lies polluted under its inhabitants; for they have transgressed laws, violated statutes, broken the everlasting covenant' (Isaiah 24.5, NRSV). And the symbolic expression of this damage is the sign that 'the wine dries up, the vine languishes' (Isaiah 24.7, NRSV).

Isaiah refers to the eternal covenant, the bond which exists between God and all that God has created. Barker points out that in the worship of the Old Testament, 'since the Temple was the microcosm of creation, the temple ritual to renew the covenant also renewed the creation'. And blood was the means by which the covenant was renewed on the Day of Atonement: 'For the life of the flesh is in the blood; and I have given it to you for making atonement for your lives upon the altar' (Leviticus 17.11, NRSV). It seems as though blood as the expression of life gives to the covenant a transfusion of new energy by which the relational ordering of creation is renewed, joy is restored, and wine is again poured out in abundance, reversing the effects of the pollution that Isaiah had identified.

It is in this context that the comment recorded by Matthew at the Last Supper makes sense: 'From now on, I tell you, I shall never again drink wine until the day I drink the new wine with you in the kingdom of my Father' (Matthew 26.29, NJB). The wine that Jesus shares at the table of his last meal is the sign of the blood that will renew the eternal covenant. From that atonement comes the renewal of all that God has created, and the new wine that is the joyful expression of all that has been healed and restored is also what the communicants drink at the eucharistic meal.

But there is one further detail that links the sensation of taste with the Last Supper and the atoning sacrifice in which Jesus sheds his blood in the restoration of the eternal covenant. All four Gospels refer to sour wine (vinegar) close to the moment of the death of Jesus. Margaret Barker finds an allusion to this in a document, the 'Letter of Barnabas', that gives evidence of early Christian thinking about the relationship between the Day of Atonement and the celebration of the Eucharist. In this letter the author maintains that the inner parts of the goat of the Old Testament sin offering (see Leviticus 16) were consumed raw (not burnt as in Leviticus) with sour wine, and he goes on to connect this with the Gospel reference to vinegar at the crucifixion. The author also quotes a text that Barker suggests belonged originally to an early Christian liturgy: 'When I am about to offer my body for the sins of this new people of mine, you will be giving me gall and sour wine to drink.'

There is something particularly striking about the connection of sour wine with the process of atonement for the pollution of sin and damage to the covenant and creation. The sense of taste alerts us to a variety of sensations. Some things naturally taste bitter and possibly unpleasant, but in other instances the bitterness is a sign of being rotten. The recognition of sour wine in the atonement sacrifice is a sensational statement about the polluting effects of sinfulness in the whole of creation. All this Jesus consumes, devouring the rottenness, cleansing the woundedness and revealing through his passion the wholeness of a renewed creation.

Not very far removed from this is the sense of passion as desire, driven by what St Augustine described as burning for the God who had touched him so profoundly. And here the language of eating is a metaphor not unfamiliar to lovers, as we recognized in the Song of Songs. But this is also language that is applied to the Eucharist, itself a love feast, and done in a way that spectacularly reverses our perception of who is consumed in the passion that seeks total identification one with another through the medium of taste.

An astonishing expression of this perception is to be found in the thirteenth-century writing of the Flemish mystic, Hadewijch, who belonged to the women's movement of her day as a Beguine, living a consecrated life but not in enclosure. In one of her poems she writes of the anguish and madness of a love that devours, exemplified in the invitation to love that we receive from Jesus who gives us himself to eat. She then continues:

> By this he made known to us
> That love's most intimate union
> Is through eating, tasting, and seeing interiorly.
> He eats us; we think we eat him,
> And we do eat him, of this we can be certain.
> But because he remains so undevoured,
> And so untouched, and so undesired,

> Each of us remains uneaten by him
> And separated so far from each other.

Hadewijch catches exactly the significance of taste, desire and union that we have been exploring in this chapter and that is at the heart of the Eucharist on Maundy Thursday. There, all the rottenness of our lives is consumed by a passion that is greater than we can comprehend. The sensation is unnerving, perhaps, and the hesitations that our pride and guilt propose indicate the extent to which we become incapable of devouring, touching, desiring, and therefore incapable of communion with each other.

For further reflection . . .

The Eucharist and communion

One of the ten modern martyrs commemorated on the west front of Westminster Abbey is Archbishop Oscar Romero. He was shot while celebrating the Eucharist in a hospital chapel.

Andrew Chandler lived in Guatemala, alongside the persecution that befell the Church in El Salvador in the late 1970s and early 1980s. In his book, *The Terrible Alternative: Christian Martyrdom in the Twentieth Century*, he describes his discovery of how the Eucharist was a statement of identification with the suffering and witness of those beyond our sight, but within the tangible companionship of table fellowship at the altar.

Communion is not only what we receive; it is the companion – one of those who break bread together – that we thereby become with receivers throughout the world.

- How real is your sense of sharing an identity with those who suffer starvation, bloodshed and humiliation when you approach the altar?
- Would participation in the Eucharist commit you to companionship with those who choose death rather than betrayal?
- What does betrayal of communion with persecuted Christians look like? Would the persecuted Church ever be justified in thinking that betrayal looks like us?

The Eucharist and the family

There are many reasons why the Eucharist should be the family service of the Church. Inclusivity is the most obvious one, since the Eucharist defines the family of the Church that is commissioned to gather around one table the peoples of the human race.

A safe environment in which human dignity is nurtured, hard lessons learned and behaviour corrected, would be another aspect of this gathering's family identity.

- What value do you attach to the care of the environment as an expression of the eucharistic offering of its fruits and the methods we use to produce and harvest them?
- Do you know where the fruit and vegetables come from that you buy in your supermarket?
- What are the conditions in those countries under which the produce you buy is grown?
- Do you buy fairly traded goods in preference to others?
- How would you describe the culture and environment of your eucharistic community?
- How might it need to change? How can you contribute constructively and patiently to that change?

Taste: Maundy Thursday

The Eucharist and atonement

The Eucharist is God's act of healing. It restores our relationships with God, with each other, with creation. In this
respect it is a source of refreshment, a well-spring.

The notions of covenant on which this meal is founded
imply that we move into a relationship that is characterized
by freedom, trust and love. It has everything of the nature of
a marriage bond about it, and takes us to the core language
of lovers (the Song of Songs is an obvious example) that we
might find disconcerting.

- How do you prepare for the Eucharist, and how do you
  give thanks afterwards?
- What does participation say to you about how you regard
  yourself?
- How do you relate to others in your eucharistic community?
- Which people annoy you? Do you recognize yourself in
  them? Does that mean that you do not like yourself very
  much?
- Are you convinced that God loves you?

For a group . . .

1. Scripture reading
   1 Kings 19.1–18.
   John 21.1–19.

In these readings we are presented with food that has something extraordinary about it. How do these stories articulate
something of memory, failure, choice and future mission? Do
the images of the hiddenness of God express ways in which
we also experience God's revelation?

2. Food and film

Either collectively or individually the group might prepare some food, and say something about the origins of the ingredients used, the method of cooking, of any symbolism associated with it.

This could also be done simply by bringing a favourite fruit or vegetable and saying something about its attractive quality, as grounds for thanksgiving, and recognition of the good desire that God satisfies in us.

The sequence from *When Harry Met Sally* may prove to be a stronger experience of cinema than the group would find comfortable. In which case, there is also an interesting comment on desire and our inability to satisfy it without reference to God in the early section of *The Life of David Gale*, starring Kevin Spacey and Kate Winslet. Both are available on DVD.

3. Serious about food

Questions for discussion:

- Lent is a time for fasting: have you as a parish ever undertaken this discipline? Do you understand the rules for doing so? (N.B. Fasting is more than giving up sweets or alcohol for a day.)
- Is there a particular cause, as a means of sanctification and expression of your communion with other Christians, for which you would offer such a Lenten discipline? Would there be a practical expression of this spiritual discipline?
- What do you think about fast food, our contemporary eating habits, and their impact on society?
- Is your parish interested in Fair Trade? Does international interest inhibit engagement with local issues that may be costly in terms of personal and collective commitment?
- How do these questions connect with your celebration of

the institution of the Eucharist and the command of
mutual love at the Mass of the Lord's Supper on Maundy
Thursday?

Reflection

Love bade me welcome: yet my soul drew back,
    Guiltie of dust and sinne.
But quick-ey'd Love, observing me grow slack
    From my first entrance in,
Drew nearer to me, sweetly questioning,
    If I lacked any thing.

A guest, I answer'd, worthy to be here:
    Love said, You shall be he.
I the unkinde, ungratefull? Ah my deare,
    I cannot look on thee.
Love took my hand, and smiling did reply,
    Who made the eyes but I?

Truth Lord, but I have marr'd them: let my shame
    Go where it doth deserve.
And know you not, sayes Love, who bore the blame?
    My deare, then I will serve.
You must sit down, sayes Love, and taste my meat;
    So I did sit and eat.

                    (George Herbert)

3

Touch: Good Friday

After Jesus had taken the wine he said, 'It is fulfilled';
and bowing his head he gave up his spirit.

(John 19.30, NJB)

Kiss and tell

One summer, when I was living in north Norfolk, on a particularly hot day I hastily pulled out of the drawer shorts
and a T-shirt and headed for the beach. On my way, I ran
into a very formidable local resident and his equally
respectable wife. They greeted me more disapprovingly than
usual, and it was only later in the day that I discovered what
the text was on my T-shirt: 'Kiss me quick . . . and squeeze
me slowly'. The accompanying artwork defies description.

Touch is something of which we are often uncertain, and
as a nation the British have tended to be rather distant and
formal in the way we greet each other. But in the course of
my lifetime the expectations of when one might embrace
another person have changed considerably. Like many of our
European neighbours, we are often more relaxed about the
exchange of a kiss or embrace when we meet.

The combination of kiss and embrace is not unfamiliar
in the Christian tradition. It is drawn from a verse of the
psalms that has been regarded as a prophetic statement
about the union of earth and heaven in the incarnation:
'Mercy and truth are met together, righteousness and

peace have kissed each other' (Psalm 85.10, BCP). This statement was celebrated in a medieval pageant entitled 'The Parliament of Heaven' in which four daughters of God, personifications of mercy, truth, justice and peace (all feminine nouns in Latin), find their conflicting claims reconciled through the birth of Jesus. The message of the pageant was that in the body of Jesus we find a statement about the kiss and embrace by heaven of the earth.

Here, where the divine and the eternal touch the human and the finite, it is to the body and embodiment, as in the last chapter on taste, that our exploration of a particular sense turns once more. This is perhaps what we should expect, since from at least the time of Aristotle the sense of taste has been identified as a tactile variant of the sense of touch. Aristotle himself further identifies touch as something that has a universal quality. This is the only sense that an animal cannot live without, that we have 'just for the sake of being; the others we have for the sake of well-being'.

The notion of the body as an organ of touch directs our attention to the body of Jesus and what statement it makes about the human experience that the incarnation redeems. By the very claim that God in Jesus inhabits a body like ours we are making a statement about a shared experience, a statement about that which we have 'for the sake of being'. So it is that God experiences our sense of hot and cold, of weightedness and bodily containment within the laws of physics and biology, of the impact of what is unyielding and solid in contrast with the comfort of what is soft, warm and safe.

Here the example of Mary is again instructive for how we might seek to understand the mystery of the body of Jesus. In one of the cycles of medieval mystery plays, the discovery that Mary is pregnant is discussed and contested by those

49

who are ignorant of her virginity. Cindy L. Carson makes
the observation that in this dramatic episode of red-hot
gossip, 'what was internal to the body becomes externalized
and impure' (*Constructions of Widowhood and Virginity in
the Middle Ages*). Mary is put on trial, and with the help of a
medieval truth drug the miraculous nature of what has happened to her is revealed so that the expectations of the world
are subverted. 'Judges are confounded, midwives are less
than wise women, detractors feel the sting of their own
words.'

The expectations of the world are not only confounded by
the mysterious character of the conception and birth of
Jesus in embodiment that touches life as we touch life; they
are also confounded by his death. St Paul reminds us that
what we preach is the body of Jesus on the cross. This is 'to
the Jews an obstacle that they cannot get over, to the gen-
tiles foolishness, but to those who have been called, whether
they are Jews or Greeks, a Christ who is both the power of
God and the wisdom of God' (1 Corinthians 1.23–24, NJB).

In all three areas of the Gospel story – conception, birth,
death – God touches life through embodiment, in the universal experience of those that God has created and in that
experience opening up new possibilities beyond it. Fifty
years on from St Paul's letter to Corinth, St Ignatius of
Antioch also identifies this 'hidden wisdom'. In a letter to
the Ephesians, St Ignatius recognizes 'the virginity of Mary
and her child-bearing and likewise also the death of the
Lord (as) three mysteries to be cried aloud, which were
made in the silence of God'. This is the Christian take on a
cosmic 'Kiss and tell'.

The image of the body of Jesus on the cover of this book
raises similar issues about our shared experience of touch.
The interior reality of the life of Jesus is both hidden and
revealed by the external reality of encounter with him. The

reality of obedience, fulfilment of the scriptures and resurrection are all externalized, and, as it were, put on trial in the discussion that takes place on the journey to Emmaus. Embodied in a reality that Cleopas and his companion also inhabit, Jesus subsequently sits at their supper table, exhibiting in Caravaggio's painting a commonality with them as he presides over the meal table, enabling them to recognize his presence by his words and actions.

But more penetratingly, Jesus touches his companions by their own recollection of how he had shaped an awareness of what was happening around them, releasing the declaration, 'Did not our hearts burn within us as he talked to us on the road and explained the scriptures to us?' (Luke 24.32, NJB). In Lent, we seek to place ourselves in the position of the disciples at Emmaus. We search out opportunities to recollect the touch of the presence of Jesus upon our lives, and find in the articulation of that recollection, perhaps with others, the renewal lovingly and hiddenly wrought by the burning presence of God within. This search will take us to the limits of ourselves.

Touching our limits

The celebration of Maundy Thursday that we explored through the sense of taste and the experience of Good Friday that we are considering through touch, are closely related. Our attention is drawn from one to the other as we focus on the body of Jesus, expressed most graphically and obviously in the giving of communion at the liturgy of the Passion on Good Friday.

How does God pursue us to the limits, into the darkest reaches of our self-abandonment to pride, superficiality and wretchedness in order to effect release in the beauty of perfection? How does the divine touch of our lives startle and disturb us so that we seek the boundaries at which transformation by the Holy Spirit enlarges and enriches us beyond our imagining?

As the season of Lent progresses, we seek to become more attuned to the location of our boundaries as the points at which the divine life touches us. The growth of this awareness is like the search for another self within, bearing the contours of our external self, but free from its constraints and imperfections, only touching the external self at certain moments and in certain places. That touch would be like connection with an electrical current in the release of energy that makes possible a spark of light or the disturbance of a sound. Hesitantly but with fascination we seek to effect this touch, to understand it, to rediscover it. We seek to direct our bodies into places, postures, moods and situations in which the inner life connects. We learn with sorrow and dismay of the ways in which other actions, thoughts or circumstances over which we have no power inevitably and against our wishes insulate us from the touch of the divine life within. These are the facts of life that threaten the vitality and meaning of our existence because they isolate us from what is eternal. The keeping of Lent as a time in which we experience hardship is readily understood.

At a popular level, this is quite widely known to be the time when we give up something, and that will probably be something that we are well known for liking. The smoker regularly seen on the street outside the office, the person who always has a bottle of wine open, but doesn't drink to excess, and the chocoholic or pudding addict are all people who have the privilege of having something to give up as a matter of choice.

Some demonstrably good things might come from such a discipline. The money saved might go to a good cause. Health and fitness might be improved. You might lose weight, or ease yourself out of a habit that was oppressive.

But one of the fundamental aspects of such a discipline must also be the sheer experience of freely chosen hardship directed towards the goal of spiritual growth. This is one of the most significant aspects of how we seek to manage the body in order to touch the life that is within. What the chosen path of hardship might be is secondary. What matters is the following of that path into an unknown territory in which we give away something we do not need in order to find something we cannot live without.

This is very close to a saying of St Isaac the Syrian that was quoted at my interview for theological college and that I have never forgotten: 'The ladder which leads to the kingdom is hidden within your own soul. Flee from sin, dive into yourself, and in your soul you will find the stairs by which to ascend.' Do not take this to mean that smoking, drinking, or sweets are necessarily sinful in themselves, but the principle of detachment is what strikes me as so similar to Isaac's wise perception. Fleeing and diving are both about the kind of risk-laden movements of transition that contain little of the sense of the ordinary and everyday, but much of the exceptional in the commitment of every bit of energy and will to whatever lies at the outcome. Such is the path of self-denial. It is a body thing, a connection enterprise that seeks to touch the divine ladder of life on which angels freely clamber up and down.

Lenten discipline can thus be very tangible, like breaking into cold water, or hitting the ground in the pounding rhythm of flight, one foot after the other pacing along the path by which attraction to temporal fancies is circumscribed and contained. The demanding struggle of this containment is imaginatively outlined in a medieval document that describes the life and conditions in which the Lady Julian lived in her anchorite cell in Norwich. The *Ancren Riwle*, a Rule for Anchorites, understands that out of the narrow containment of such an experience comes revelation. The *Riwle* makes a play on the word 'Mary', which also means 'bitter' in Hebrew. It states, 'Then should you in a narrow place endure "bitterness", as Jesus did in Mary's womb, when you are confined within four walls, and he in a narrow cradle – nailed to the cross – and in the tomb of stone closely confined. Mary's womb and this tomb were his anchorite cell.'

Although in terms of detail the life of withdrawal is an exceptional vocation, Lent is a reminder of the degree to which there is an exceptional element in the universal vocation of all Christians. In this regard it is an outworking and renewing of the decisive moments of touch, of transformation and of the commitment of Christian initiation that will be renewed at Easter in the culmination of this six-week programme of exploration.

Here we are confronted by the containment of the 'cradle' of the cross as the location of our re-birth in Christ. The image of water is to be found here also. First, it is in the touch that pierces the side of Christ to release water and blood, the symbols of sacramental life, evoking the images of the older covenant experience with the piercing of the rock in the desert (Exodus 17.1–7). Second, it is in the bitterness of the water that signifies the struggle of a pilgrim people to live within the narrowness of God's provision (Exodus 15.22–25). And third, it is found in the image of the womb/tomb, evoked by the font from which we emerge as people of the new creation, born again by water and the Spirit (Romans 6.3–4).

Through this exploration of our capacity to reach the liminal boundaries of our lives we should expect to recover some greater sense of ourselves and the scope of divine life within. Somewhere in this location the feet of the ladder to heaven stand. The point at which they touch the ground of our life is the point of baptismal encounter, where angels minister and heaven opens to us (Genesis 28.10–17; John 1.47–51). This touch reveals not only the manifestation of the glory of God, but also our own identity.

Touching the silence

A remarkable episode of touch and revelation is recorded in Mark 5.21–43. It is a double story; the healing of the woman with the issue of blood is told within the story of the raising of the daughter of Jairus. How does touch function as a medium of revelation, delivering that spark of light by which truth is revealed in the shadowland of our experience?

In the main story, about the daughter of Jairus, it is Jesus who responds to a request for help and takes the initiative. He takes the girl by the hand, awakens her to life, and calls for food to renew her strength. This touch brings new life, revealing the power of Jesus as the word through whom all things came into existence. But the context of this revealing is also important. It happens within the company of the nascent Church – Peter, James and John – and is a sign of the mystery of the kingdom of God, the revealing of something that has an interior and hidden quality about it; 'he gave them strict orders not to let anyone know about it' (Mark 5.43, NJB).

This quality of hiddenness and revelation is also marked in the story that intercepts the journey to the house of Jairus. Here Jesus is passive, and it is the woman who touches his person through the symbol of his clothing. This we might read as clothing that has a vestment-like quality to it. As the means by which the invisible God becomes visible, the clothing of embodiment is the vesture in which, in the words of a hymn by St Ephrem the Syrian, we are called to recognize Jesus:

The First-born wrapped himself in a body
As a veil to hide his glory.
The immortal Bridegroom shines out in that robe:
Let the guests in their clothing resemble him in his.

This is a perception drawn from the book of Hebrews that is echoed in a more familiar hymn referring to Jesus as 'robed in flesh, our great High Priest'. But the revealing of the identity of Jesus is not the central focus of what is accomplished in this touch. The dramatic force of the story is in the revealing of the relationship that the woman has with Jesus. A bond of faith that he recognizes internally only becomes manifest when she takes material form by emerging from the anonymity of the crowd to be recognized as the person who touched him. 'He continued to look all around to see who had done it. Then the woman came forward, frightened and trembling because she knew what had happened to her' (Mark 5.32–33, NJB).

Both these stories provide powerful images that illustrate the complexity and bewilderment of coming to faith and Christian discipleship. What is within us does not remain hidden when we touch the life of Jesus. The moments of our encounter with that life, indwelling us through the power of the Holy Spirit, reveal us in ways that may be bewildering and uncomfortable. Ask any priest or lay Christian involved in public ministry, no matter how low or high the profile of that ministry might be, about just how uncomfortable it can be. When, to use our earlier analogy, the current of electrical power that is divine life connects, there is a flash of light or a sound, and it disturbs.

This flash of disturbance is the mystery wrought in the silence of God that St Ignatius described as needing to be 'cried aloud'. In the rites of Christian initiation (baptism, confirmation and communion) the sign of the laying-on of hands is a statement of touch that carries with it the under-taking to become the Church that cries aloud the mystery of who Jesus is and who we are. The whole people of God is the body that must speak and celebrate the mystery of this transforming truth.

In Peter Weir's film, *Dead Poets Society*, John Keating, played by Robin Williams, is an unconventional and charismatic English master at a prestigious academy in the United States. At one critical point in the film Mr Keating asks his pupils to write a poem that will be read out in their next lesson. Todd Anderson struggles with the task of composition, fails and has to admit in the next lesson that he hasn't written anything. Why?

The analysis from Mr Keating is incisive and widely applicable even to those who have left behind teenage adolescence. 'Mr Anderson thinks that everything inside him is worthless and embarrassing.' Getting Todd up on to the dais in front of the class, Mr Keating cajoles a response from him. He lays hands on the boy's head to cover his eyes, and then prompting, goading and encouraging him, he elicits more and more as Todd unleashes from inside himself a creative force that has astonishing eloquence and imagination.

This episode has the force of a parable about Christian vocation, and the humility and confidence needed to move on from the spiritual adolescence of guilt into a maturity that can face shame with honesty, penitence and willingness to change. 'Let your light so shine,' declares the Book of Common Prayer as the people of God offer themselves in the eucharistic sacrifice of praise and thanksgiving. But as Christians, we are not always very agile in perceiving the light of the life of Christ in ourselves, or celebrating with joy its discovery in other people.

Perhaps this is one of the reasons why there is a growing interest in the ministry of spiritual direction, particularly as a ministry undertaken with great skill by lay people. It is a work of beauty and gentleness, drawing on every type of human communication, emotion and psychological disposition. It seeks to enable recognition of the points where the Holy Spirit touches, reveals, empowers and overwhelms our sense of worthlessness and embarrassment, and consequently our silence. It is the work of being asked to view, with the eyes of Christ, humanity from the cross, and love whatever you can find that is capable of being loved in every person that you see, because that alone alleviates the agony of the passion that keeps you there.

The refreshment that we discover in the gift of a person who can minister in this place is profound, and articulated with the eloquence of that discovery in a description by the Jesuit, Javier Melloni in *The Way Supplement*, No. 103:

What is the colour of the light of your eyes,
   that you can contemplate everything before you and
     make it live?
What is the power of your breath, that your joy
   dissolves all my wounds?
What is the power of your mouth,
   that you can sculpt my innermost self into a chalice?
You accompany me wherever I go with the caress of
   your regard;
silently, you see me home into a place of rest.
Through your words, you let me hear myself; through
   your eyes, you let me see myself.
Living witness, the world sustains you, but you
   sustain the world,
and in each of your gestures you spread the Presence
   that dwells within you, pointing out to me always
   the one and only goal: the Living God.
Blessed are we if we can live in the realm of

transparency and liberty. And more blessed still if
we can speak, look, and touch with liberated
transfigured hearts.

Isolation is not the vocation to which Christians are called,
even in the extreme situation of solitary life. Touch, the
expression of embodiment, is also an essential of spiritual
growth, experienced through the companionship of another
pilgrim. When the enterprise of Christian living is tough
going, the inextinguishable life of the Holy Spirit within
another person is a reminder that we can easily lose sight of
that life within ourselves. However, recovery of contact with
the life within may also require the touch that heals and
restores, taking us by the hand and reawakening us from
sleep.

Touching the darkness

The story of the raising of Jairus's daughter uses sleep as a
metaphor for death and, I suppose, the things that we asso-
ciate with death: darkness, fear, grief, pain, loss. These are
all experiences that we encounter in a variety of ways
throughout life. They suggest moments of received or self-
inflicted hurt from which we seek the release and comfort of
being taken by the hand, awoken into an environment of
love and comfort that we thought we knew existed, and
given new strength, independence and freedom in a meal.

In 1970 a musician with a social conscience, Ralph
McTell, published a song called 'The Streets of London'.
When I was at university it already had a retrospective feel,
but the story of urban dislocation that it narrates remains
authentic. To a complaint of accidie and loneliness, the
singer tells the tale of those whose home is the streets and
responds:

So how can you tell me you're lonely
and say for you that the sun don't shine?
Let me take you by the hand
and lead you through the streets of London,
show you something to make you change your mind.

To be led by the hand through the streets of London today may well be a prospect that many people would find alarming, especially if it included an encounter with those who live on them. But such encounters, in London or any big city, also provide a challenge to find revelation at the limits of our experience. Ralph McTell's song is associated in my mind with much that was compelling in the articulation of the social gospel.

The second verse of Ralph McTell's song tells of an old woman with dirt in her hair and her clothes in rags, 'carrying her home in two carrier bags'. How that woman came to be on the streets we do not know. But the image of her connects in my mind very vividly with the life and work of an amazing Christian woman who combined the discipline of the faith that had formed her in the first half of the twentieth century with the need for its fresh expression in the social gospel and other ways in the second half. Her name was Sr Lorna Mary of the Society of St Margaret, with whom I was enormously privileged to work as curate in Leicester.

Sr Lorna was a nurse and a religious sister through and through. Her habit bulged with all kinds of useful bits of stuff that meant she was never lost for a safety pin, plaster, aspirins, string, scissors, pens, paper, prayer book, rosary, crucifix, etc. Her love for those in need was practical and profound, enlivened by an unsentimental and anticipatory awareness of the holy. I used to accompany her to the local home for blind people every Sunday afternoon in order to celebrate the Eucharist; there was no doubt who was in charge! She was confident in her management of the home as holy ground.

On the journeys to and from the home I learnt a lot about the heroic work of the Society of St Margaret, especially at the Hostel of God in Clapham, where Sr Lorna had worked for many years. It was essentially a forerunner of what we know as the hospice movement and had been founded in 1896 as the Free Home for the Dying. This was a place to which people were taken who had nowhere else to go to die; they were the people that London had discarded.

Sr Lorna told me the story of giving a bath on one occasion to a woman in the Hostel of God whose body was wasted by a life in prostitution and who was very close to death. As Sr Lorna washed and dried the much-used body with great care, the woman inhabiting it said to her, 'Sister, you're the first person who has ever touched me.' It was a memorable statement. It issued from somewhere deep within a woman who had spent her life, from what early stage one can only guess, allowing men, for a negotiated sum of money, to touch her in intimate and degrading ways. This had been a means, possibly enforced by circumstance, of earning her living and securing at least a chimera of independence and pride. What permanent invasion of her dignity had resulted, again, we can only guess.

But perhaps the recognition that dignity had not been entirely effaced came with the unmistakable experience of a touch that took nothing but gave so much by way of restoration. Led by the hand of God into a distinctive vocation, Sr Lorna was herself the expression of the hand that would touch and restore dignity to those who had had it stolen from them on the streets of London.

The recognition of this profoundly transforming encounter must surely say something to us about the way in which we touch others. In the structured context of the liturgy, the touch of the handshake as a sign of peace has in its time caused anxiety to those asked to exchange it. I have to confess that my own English reserve has sometimes been alarmed by the enthusiasm of others around me. However, a profound statement is being made about this touch with people whom we may not know at all. It is a statement that indicates commonality, an affirmation of the raw material of humanity, and the communication of restoration and dignity implicit in all Christ-like touch.

On Good Friday the liturgy provides an opportunity for us to express the statement of commonality in the veneration of the cross. For some, this is literally a touch in the form of a kiss. For others, it is the touch of contrition that brings us, also literally, to our knees. It is a moment that conveys to us the gift of the Holy Spirit, for which the sign of touch is the normal expression in the laying-on of hands. Those who gather to be with Jesus as he is taken to the limit of the darkness of death are those to whom his spirit is handed over. 'And bowing his head he give up his Spirit' (John 19.30, NJB). The Greek word that St John uses for this is the word used for tradition. Jesus hands over his Spirit to those who stand with him at the cross. But this word for handing over also comes with the disturbing connotation of betrayal.

The challenge of the handing over of the Spirit on Good Friday presents us with stark choices. If we touch the hem of his robe, if we come to the cross, there is the danger that everything that we are will be revealed. Could you go that far? How far have you in fact already gone? In its symbolic inauguration through the imposition of ashes on Ash Wednesday, the enactment of Lent, with its disciplines and minor deaths to self-interest and indulgence, is a ritual that supposes we have embarked on the way to total revelation in which we stand before God and each other stripped of all pretence.

Touch: Good Friday

Lent is the transformation into a six-week season of a particular group identity within the life of the early Church: the group of Penitents. These were people who had in some way broken their pledge of commitment to the faith handed over to them in the solemn rites of initiation for which preparation had been detailed and lengthy. They subverted the word for tradition into the one for betrayal, thereby damaging the unity and bond of peace within the Church. Reception back into the company of the Church required enrolment in the order of Penitents. The sign of that reception was the laying-on of hands by the bishop, a symbol of touch that indicated a new release of the restorative power of the Holy Spirit.

Today we tend to deal with our betrayals rather more privately. But no less do those betrayals damage the integrity of holiness in the community of the Church, in our own lives, and in society. We also know that privacy isolates as much as it protects. In a society that experiences the interior darkness of intense loneliness, there is no one to tell, 'It hurts'. For many people, the use of the sacrament of confession has been a way of seeking the touch that reveals restoration and the opportunity to unburden ourselves of truths we cannot bare to face or cover up any longer.

In so many respects, the process of making your confession has become more pastorally sensitive to people's needs, an expression not of mechanical absolution, but of encouragement, searing honesty and joyful unburdening. I have been struck recently by the number of people who have asked to make their confession for the first time after many years of Christian discipleship. This desire and experience takes us to the judgement seat of God, before which we shall all come. Faced with the majesty and the compassion of God, we also dare to recognize the God who is within, and who knows all that we are and have done, and whom so often we

have sought, like the child wandering in the darkness looking for a parent to provide safety and reassurance.

The image of darkness re-emerges from the story of the
raising of Jairus's daughter as the context of sleep (or death)
from which we are awoken into life. Here our imagination
might allow us to think of Jesus as the one who banishes the
song of lament, and sings a new song in which he invites us
to be taken by the hand, to be led through suffering and
darkness on the journey into God and into life.

In *The Darkness of God*, a book by Denys Turner that
explores this theme in Christian mysticism, we are directed
to the writing of the great thirteenth-century Franciscan, St
Bonaventure. It is in Bonaventure's presentation of 'the
broken, crucified Christ, in a "similarity" so "dissimilar" as
to dramatize with paradoxical intensity the brokenness and
failure of all our language and knowledge of God', Turner
writes, that we find our way through the darkness into God.
The relationship between similarity and dissimilarity,
between the touch of the God within us and as us and the
search for that God, between experience of God in the flash
of inspiration and the numbness of our language when we
try to articulate the mystery of that encounter, are all con-
texts and experiences that we can describe as like searching
in the darkness.

Darkness and death are the points at which Bonaventure
ends his treatise, *The Soul's Journey into God*. It does not
conclude with any sense of despair, but the conviction that
by touching the element of death and all it represents at the
limit of our existence and knowledge, we touch and are
touched by God in the only way that is possible as the means
of access to the vision of God. This journey into the darkness
is a journey out of loneliness, a journey into company with
the dispossessed and the wretchedness of our own experience as the point at which Jesus touches us in the

universalizing experience of embodiment. It is a journey propelled by attraction to the love for us that we find at that point of narrow and bitter limitation. Here we are brought to the cross, and Bonaventure concludes:

Whoever loves this death
can see God
because it is true beyond doubt that
a *mortal will not see me and live* (Exodus 33.20).
Let us, then, die
and enter into the darkness;
let us impose silence upon our cares, our desires and our imaginings.
With Christ crucified
let us pass *out of this world to the Father* (John 13.1)
so that when the Father is shown to us,
we may say with Philip:
It is enough for us (John 14.8).
Let us hear with Paul:
My grace is sufficient for you. (2 Corinthians 12.9)
Let us rejoice with David saying:
My flesh and my heart have grown faint;
You are the God of my heart,
and the God that is my portion for ever.
Blessed be the Lord forever
and all the people will say:
Let it be; let it be.
Amen. (Psalm 73.26; 106.48)

For further reflection . . .

Laying hands on our intentions
Lent is a time for reaching our limits. This means, inevitably, reaching parts of our lives that are easily neglected, parts

that we prefer not to encounter, and parts that are so remote to us that we rarely attempt to connect with them.

Like a pilgrim who had walked to Compostella and declared, 'I had come to an end of myself', the journey of Lent that takes us to Good Friday and the cross, takes us to the part of our lives of which we are probably most afraid: our death.

- How is your Lenten discipline going? Do you need to adjust your expectations, or be humble and brave in starting up again?
- Giving up something for Lent is a small death; confident of finding that what you value most is held in God's hands, how much else on earth are you ready to part with?
- In the desert, God gives his people springs of water: what forms of spiritual refreshment and delight have you discovered in the desert of this Lent, and your Christian pilgrimage so far?

Laying hands on our life

Lent is not a closed season, in the sense that it is self-contained. There is an unhurried and steady joy in its character as a season of solemn preparation. The longer season of Easter (50 days) is not the reversal of Lent, but its fulfilment.

This preparation is space in a busy world for re-connection with God's gifts to us, the gift of baptism most obviously of all, as we die and rise with Christ.

- What are your stories of encounter with God? Are you familiar with the details? How often do you stop to ask yourself that question? Where do you find time for reflection on this aspect of your life?

- Why might you believe, like Todd Anderson in *Dead Poets' Society*, that your experience of faith and your powers of communication are not worth much?
- The telling is, in itself, a beautiful process of discovery; is there a wise person that you know and trust who would listen to your story?

Laying hands on our hurts

The hurt of sin can be inflicted in many forms, with devastating consequences. The search for healing and restoration is not always an easy one to embark upon.

When we are distressed by our hurts, we can also confuse the source of the damage, often blaming ourselves for things we have not done, while blaming others for the equally serious things we are responsible for.

- What would an audit of your most serious hurts reveal? Can you disentangle the damage that has been done to you from the damage you have inflicted on others or on yourself?
- In the season of Lent, everyone is a penitent, to some extent; is this a time to make your confession, lay hands on your sins and take them to the cross in search of forgiveness and absolution? Do you also need to seek the touch of healing that binds the wounds of hurt inflicted by others upon you?
- Do you know a church where an experienced priest will be able to help you prepare for these sacramental signs of liberation, and celebrate them with you?

For a group . . .

1. Scripture reading
  2 Samuel 12.1–25: David's repentance.
  Luke 7.36–50: Jesus restores a woman's dignity.
These stories reflect something of the ambiguity and mixture of signs and motives that surround the damaged areas of our lives. In both instances the symbols of penitence and grief draw healing and new life from God's hand.

2. Touch and film
Members of the group bring with them something (a photograph or other item such as a letter, gift or memento) that represents a sinful or wounded aspect of life, either in their own experience or in the world. Each person presents the object, places it in the centre of the group and tells the story attached it. The leader of the group then directs a time of silence, perhaps some simple prayer for healing; the group might say one of the penitential psalms (Psalm 32, 51 or 130, for example). This concludes with someone else returning the object to its owner and making some simple statement of encouragement or thanks for sharing their experience.

The sequence from the film *Dead Poets' Society* is one possible viewing in this section. So also is a sequence from the film *The Mission*, starring Jeremy Irons and Robert de Niro. The sequence follows Mendoza's penance of carrying his slave-trading arms and weapons up to the Jesuit mission territory, to be released from them by the Guarani, whom he had previously hunted. Both are available on DVD.

3. Kiss and tell
Questions for discussion:
- What aspects of your shared keeping of Lent are you finding most helpful, or most difficult? Why is this so?

Touch: Good Friday

- Looking at a map of the area that your parish covers, what are the points at which you variously touch the life of the local community, or the wider society beyond your parish boundary? How and by whom is that contact made?
- What opportunities do you have for marking in liturgical celebration or other ways the events that touch people's lives most profoundly – birth, marriage, death?
- What place does confession – the sacrament of reconciliation – and the ministry of healing have in your life as a Christian community? How could it be celebrated more obviously and inclusively?
- How might the liturgy of Good Friday reflect something of your keeping of Lent this year?

Reflection
From *The Dialogue* of St Catherine of Siena (1347–1380):

Then eternal Truth seized her desire and drew it more strongly to himself. Just as in the Old Testament when sacrifice was offered to God a fire came and drew to God the sacrifice that was acceptable, so gentle Truth did to that soul of hers. He sent the fiery mercy of the Holy Spirit and seized the sacrifice of desire she had made of herself, saying to her:

No virtue can have life in it except from charity, and charity is nursed and mothered by humility. You will find humility in the knowledge of yourself when you see that even your own existence comes not from yourself but from me, for I loved you before you came into being. And with unutterable love for you I willed to create you anew in grace. So I washed you and made you a new creation in the blood of the only-begotten Son poured out with such burning love.

4

Smell: Holy Saturday

They took the body of Jesus, wrapped it with the spices in
linen cloths, according to the burial custom of the Jews.

(John 19.40, NJB)

Smell and recollection

My school tuck box has been around a bit, and is still doing
good service supporting the pending tray and various other
types of invaluable storage space in my study. This means
that access to the tuck box itself is only very rarely possible,
and there is advantage to this. When opened, it is like a
Pandora's Box of smells and attendant memories that are
increasingly a fond distraction.

The overriding smell is that of putrefaction, something
that never bothered me in the brief period of my life at
boarding school. Tuck boxes were located in the cellars of the
boarding house and provided one of the few areas of private,
padlocked space for storage of things that really mattered.
What drove our pre-adolescent interest in such privacy was,
as I recall, the stockpiling of food, especially sweet things
regarded by the authorities as unsuitable. It didn't matter to
us that Jaffa Cakes turned green, jellies became rocklike,
and treacle, for which there was a craze in my second year,
seeped into and coated the other contents of the tuck box –
playing cards, marbles, letters from home and those jour-
nals strictly forbidden and hugely coveted: comics.

What really did torment us, however, was the knowledge that at any moment, with no warning, there could be an inspection by the headmaster's wife, cheerfully accompanied by matron (who was supposed to be our friend). Both of them had the unquestionable authority to command us to open the tuck box and clear out its treasured contents if they fell outside acceptable standards. That those standards might have existed in order to preserve our own health and safety never occurred to us. The raid was invariably painful and punitive. Perhaps my later association of the tuck box with the pending tray of adult life was formed in that distant childhood experience. But when, on rare occasions I clear sufficient space to open the tuck box, the faint smell of treasured sweet and rotting things conjures up a deeply submerged delight and the fear of unexpected inspection.

My indulgence in this recollection is offered simply in order to provide evidence for the claim that smell is a sense that evokes the past. This sense enables us to unlock chambers in our memory that may remain impenetrable to other intellectual and sensory stimuli. Perhaps it is for this reason that smell is so closely associated with the establishment of the covenant that God makes with Noah after the flood. This covenant is universal ('between God and every living creature on earth', Genesis 9.17, NJB) and eternal (times and seasons 'will never cease', Genesis 8.22, NJB). It is established by the burnt offerings that Noah offers, and 'Yahweh smelt the pleasing smell' (Genesis 8.21, NJB).

The smell of God

The author of the story of Noah seems to be drawing on human experience to make a profound statement about our understanding of the nature of God. God knows, sees into the secret places of all that God has made, and so remembers: that is to say, holds in mind all time as an eternal present, cosmically. By extension, smell, the thing that prompts our memory, can be said daringly and metaphorically to prompt the memory of God that is clearly of a wholly different order, but is intelligible to us in ways that draw on how we understand ourselves, made in God's image. The ancient originality of the statement that God smelt the pleasing smell is a startling declaration that even in the tradition of Jewish commentary on the scriptures it is regarded as disturbing because of its anthropomorphic imagery.

As with our exploration of the sense of touch, this imagery takes us again to a distinctive threshold from which we survey the future. This is a place of liminality: 'the world judgement of the Flood hangs like an iron curtain between this world age and that of the first splendour of creation', declares the Old Testament scholar, Gerhard von Rad. But it is only a curtain, a veil beyond which we do not see the prehistory that is also ours. The human race and the animal kingdom, represented by all that has been saved in the ark, emerge to face a new future. Here, all creation is bound together in covenant, and the starting point of their new life is the altar on which the smoke of sacrifice arises to God.

Although the image of the smelling and consequent remembering by God is an extreme and in many respects compelling one, von Rad does also make the point that 'there is a realm of silence and secrecy in respect to what God works in sacrifice'. God is not being presented as a deity that is wilfully angered and similarly placated. The sensation of smell is being used to describe something of the mysterious nature of God who holds in silence and secrecy (more securely than the safety of my tuck box) the content of our lives, and remembers. God as essentially one who remembers is an understanding and strand of lamentation that emerges in those psalms seeking reassurance that God has not changed or become forgetful of a people who themselves all too easily forget their creator. 'Forget not' is therefore a recurrent cry to God, balanced in Psalm 119 by the repeated declaration that we in turn will not forget the statutes or the words of God.

Alongside this tradition of psalmody in the context of Temple worship, we also have the cry of the prophets who similarly understand God as one who remembers. 'Can a woman forget her nursing child, or show no compassion for the child of her womb? Even these may forget, yet I will not forget you' (Isaiah 49.15, NRSV). It is the mother of a nursing child, Mary, who similarly proclaims the recollection of God in the thanksgiving of her *Magnificat*: 'He has helped his servant Israel, in remembrance of his mercy' (Luke 1.54, NRSV). And the connection between the recollection of mercy and the odour of worship is to be made most graphically in the event of the Epiphany, the moment at which the silent secret of God is revealed in the Christ child through the magi's gifts, of which frankincense is the potent statement of the disclosure of God.

The identification between some sense of the presence of God and the use of incense is an ancient and essentially scriptural one, closely linked with worship and the life of the Temple. The presentation of incense by one of the magi heralds the identification between Jesus and the Temple that we find in John's Gospel: 'Destroy this temple, and in three days I will raise it up . . . But he was speaking of the temple that was his body' (John 2.19, 21, NRSV). However, the connection between the Temple, incense, and the disclosure of God is not a metaphorical one.

The second book of Chronicles gives an account of the duties of the Levites that refers specifically to the offering of incense to God 'morning after morning, evening after evening' as an indication of its constant use in worship (2 Chronicles 13.11). Furthermore, in the description of the dedication of the Temple reference to the cloud that incense makes is used to represent the presence of God:

> When the song was raised, with trumpets and cymbals and other musical instruments, in praise to the LORD, 'For he is good, for his steadfast love endures forever', the house, the house of the LORD, was filled with a cloud, so that the priests could not stand to minister because of the cloud; for the glory of the LORD filled the house of God. (2 Chronicles 5.13–14, NRSV)

Here again, the connection between the fragrance of a burnt offering and the presence of God who is consistent, who never forgets, 'for his steadfast love endures for ever', is clearly made.

The point that the priests were no longer able to minister is also a statement that suggests the element of silence and mystery identified by von Rad as characteristic of the presence of God. This theme of mystery and the proper fear of what is secret or hidden is celebrated with even greater dramatic detail in the story from the exodus of the revelation of God to Moses on Mount Sinai and the giving of the Ten Commandments. Here, it is the people who are called to remember the sensory experience of the cloud and the extravagant, awe-inspiring worship. We can only wonder at the ceremonies that might have been undertaken to provoke the description of thunder pealing and lightning flashing, and the smoke of censers being enough to cover a mountain.

Moses speaks reassuringly to the people of Israel about the purpose of the liturgy that they have witnessed at a critical moment of their pilgrimage. His words are translated in this way in the King James Version of the Bible: 'Fear not: for God is come to prove you, and that his fear may be before your faces, that ye sin not' (Exodus 20.20). The phrase, 'that his fear may be before your faces' may strike us curious, but it is a statement of recollection that has found literal expression in the liturgical ordering of many Anglican churches, perhaps most obviously and ubiquitously in the City of London and Wren's designs for the rebuilding of places of worship after the great fire of 1666.

Behind the simple altar tables of the late seventeenth and early eighteenth centuries one is likely still to find a highly ornamented wooden reredos on which is written the text of the Commandments laid upon the children of Israel within the liturgy that celebrated and subsequently recollected God's presence in their midst. As congregations in the City of London faced the east wall of their newly rebuilt churches, the words handed down on Sinai confronted them as a statement of recollection, the fear of God being evoked before their faces. But the statement was more than visual; this was also the context in which recollection of the revealing of God in the action of bringing about the world's salvation was liturgically enacted.

This recollection took place when the Eucharist was celebrated, with the people of God having 'in remembrance' the death and Passion of Jesus as they became 'partakers of his most blessed body and blood'. Here no clouds of incense accompanied their worship, as far as we know, but the context in which it was located as an act of remembering is one that reeks scripturally and metaphorically of the worship of the Temple that was fulfilled in the perfect sacrifice of Jesus. Not surprisingly, it has seemed entirely appropriate to subsequent generations of worshippers that it should also reek literally, as we keep before our faces – and senses – the fear of the Lord that smell and the cloud of incense provoke. Mindful of the location of this experience in the pilgrimage history of the people of Israel, we might also enquire into what the symbolic impact of the cloud might be on our own generation.

We tend to be a people that proceed with a high level of forgetfulness of the past, but an equally high level of response to sensory stimulus in the search for experience of what we term spiritual in the here and now. How might the sense of smell function to direct our journey towards a recollection of the God of silence and mystery? In Jesus Christ this God has breathed the scent of our life and history; now his tomb opens like the fissure in the desert rock to disclose before us the water of new life that is ours for eternity. The journey to the dawning light has its own opacity. Three novels by Rose Macaulay capture something of its quality, the first of them set in a more recent episode in the history of the City of London.

The smell of mortality

Like the great fire of 1666, the bombing of London still haunts many, in some cases through the memory of those who experienced it. Herbert Mason's famous photograph taken from the roof of Northcliffe House on 29 December 1940 shows St Paul's standing defiantly amid the smoke and wreckage of the blitz and is one of the most popular images of the last century.

Rose Macaulay, a literary and intellectual figure who lived through that upheaval, uses the metaphor of recollected childhood to describe the consequences of that dislocation. Her novel, *The World My Wilderness*, is an exploration of the experience of loss and the deep sense of a quest for something that belongs to us on the other side of a boundary that we do not quite know how to cross. Macaulay enters the territory of this theme through the description of exile and the dislocated family life of the main character, a teenage girl called Barbary. We explore the consequent disruption of habit and stability, and are given an insight into the interior wasteland of all the characters in the novel that is externally represented by the bombed-out area around St Paul's Cathedral.

The final chapter presents us with an intriguing range of symbolic representation. At one level 'mess and smashed things' seems to be 'an earnest, perhaps, of the universal doom'. But in the midst of 'the broken city . . . michaelmas daisies, milky ways of tiny blue stars, crowded among the withered rose-bay, the damp brown bracken, the sprawling nightshade and the thistles'. These signs of life that emerge from deep within the earth are what Macaulay describes as the wilderness, a term that is used not in the sense of desert, but of untamed, untilled, rich potential.

The wild plants are manifestations of the forces of nature that in Barbary's dysfunctional family life were being smothered, just as the dysfunctional buildings and structures destroyed by bombing stood on wilderness ground that yielded wild fruits and scented weeds. As cranes and scaffolding moves in for the rebuilding of the city, the bonfires on which the weeds were burnt yield 'dreams of memory' in blue smoke, 'smelling of incense and autumn' and redolent of something described by Gerard Manley Hopkins as 'the dearest freshness deep down things' in contrast to the surface stuff that 'wears man's smudge and shares man's smell'.

Macaulay does not write from a conventional Christian viewpoint, and in many ways her questioning is resonant with the culture of our own time, half a century later. In her later novel, *The Towers of Trebizond*, similar themes of enquiry, mystery and journeying into the unknown also emerge. Towards the end of a novel that also has an autobiographical ring to it, the main character, Laurie, makes the observation that most of her friends are not Christians, but are interested in churches and the history of religion. She goes on to reveal something that is also a recurrent theme in her novels, a love affair, and the source of an unresolved

tension in her spiritual journey: 'I had come between Vere
and his wife for ten years; he had given me his love, mental
and physical, and I had taken it . . . Vere always said that
he was fonder of her because of me; men are given to saying
this.'

The tragedy for Laurie is that Vere is killed in a car crash
while she is driving. Here Macaulay writes from what one
feels can only be the devastation of personal experience,
although as an English scholar she vents her grief through
the medium of a quotation from John Davies of Hereford's
dirge for his friend Thomas Morley, in which one suspects
Macaulay finds the articulation of a love that, like her own,
may not easily have been afforded social recognition or
borne with dignity:

> Death has deprived me of my dearest friend,
> My dearest friend is dead and laid in the grave.
> In grave he rests until the world shall end,
> The world shall end, as end all things must have.

Believing herself to be in some way outside the acceptable
boundaries of the institutional Church, Macaulay seeks the
inchoate memory of some part of her that cannot be
detached from God and might be found through the language of symbol. The

> liturgical words and music (were) like fine architecture
> being reared up into the sky . . . and the rows of candles
> lifted their flames like yellow tulips, and the incense
> flowed about us . . . And sometimes the doors would
> swing ajar, and there the kingdom was, clear and terrible
> and bright, and no Church is able for it, or can do more
> than grope.

Macaulay's description reminds us not only of the majesty of the theophany on Mount Sinai; it is also evocative of the atmosphere of Holy Saturday in which the glory of Easter is no more than a slice of light towards which we make unhurried and reflective progress.

Liturgical symbolism, words and music feature as background areas of dispute in a third novel, *They Were Defeated*. Set in Devon and Cambridge, this story takes us back to the seventeenth century, and weaves a narrative in which many of the great authors of the period feature as the century moves to its tumultuous middle years and civil war. The names of Herrick, Crawshaw, Cleveland, Marvell, Ford and Cosin all occur in the *dramatis personae* of the story that ends with another tragic, accidental death. This ghastly, swift event stands in the novel as a statement about a death that is about to befall England in the loss of its monarch and a richness of imagery in worship to which Cosin (later Bishop of Durham) and the then Archbishop of Canterbury, William Laud, had been committed.

Intellect is the theme that drives this account of a bucolic parish and academic life. At the death of the central character, the ambiguously named Julian Coneybeare, the poet John Cleveland is made to reflect in the words of his own poetry on that woman who had been his lover and, by the trick of disguising herself as a young man, his pupil. 'He had possessed her (Julian's) lovely body, but had he touched the freedom of her mind? If he had, she had regained it now, wherever her delicate virgin spirit might be straying, gravely dreaming along the gallant walks of Paradise, untroubled by such as he.'

In the three themes that emerge from Macaulay's novels, our management of creation and the environment, our human relationships, sexuality and the drift of love and hurt, and in our intellect that seeks to know what is beyond the horizon of our vision, we find material for which the liturgy of Holy Saturday provides the stimulus to remember and experience. The sense of smell connects us with the central symbol in this rite, the symbol of the cloud, used variously to describe the presence of God, and drawn from the reality of incense and its use in worship to celebrate then, as now, that presence.

What we are expressing in this symbol of the cloud is akin to the Genesis description of God through the metaphor of smelling a pleasing odour and God remembering Godself in a binding covenant. In the symbol of Holy Saturday's re-enactment of the Easter Passover sacrifice that symbolically marks our pilgrimage departure on a path from earth to heaven, we are, in the imagery of St Paul, 'under the cloud', or baptized into it (1 Corinthians 10.2, 3). In this cloud we also recollect something of how we are to be ourselves.

The scripture readings over which we pore in a night of vigil on Holy Saturday are replete with images that resonate with those promptings and starting places for a journey of exploration to the goal of our vocation and destiny: life in heaven. These readings call us to responsible stewardship of the earth (in the story of creation: Genesis 1.1–2.2), the healing of intimate relationships ('Yahweh has called you back like a forsaken, grief-stricken wife, like the repudiated wife of his youth', Isaiah 54.6, NJB) and the search for wisdom ('You have forsaken the fountain of wisdom! . . . Learn where knowledge is, where strength, where understanding . . . But who has found out where she lives, who has entered her treasure house?', Baruch 3.12, 14, 15, NJB).

The cloud, as the atmosphere in which they are read, has a significantly inclusive character to it, commanding through its quality of smell the participation of all who are enfolded within it, irrespective of any status or capacity.

Presence is the only qualification for inclusion in its release of memories about ourselves that suggest a richer connectedness than we might dare to expect. The cloud, as a metaphor for the presence of God, places us in a dimension in which it is possible to connect with the holding together of time that is characteristic of God and restores to us our past as well as our future in a dispensation that reconciles and heals as we discover our time and life held in God. The cloud is thus a way of defining an environment in which those aspects of life that are characterized by damage, loss and confusion are also enfolded or covered.

Taken into the cloud, our human and creaturely experience is not metamorphosed by divine assimilation. The cloud is, rather, a description of the context in which we travel towards the sliver of light upon the horizon that signals the glory of the resurrection and the light in which we are destined to come fully to life. Over all our hesitations and uncertainties, the cloud provides a cover.

This is how the Old Testament seems to envisage the healing power of blood as it is applied ritually in the Temple to cover the torn faith and rents of waywardness that had damaged the covenant, the blood thereby mending and renewing it. In the Temple rite of atonement, this covering gave new life to the land, healed relationships damaged by injustice, and disclosed wisdom. In a similar way, our rending of the environment, our torn and broken relationships, and what the poet Francis Thompson calls the 'benumbed conceiving' of our intellect in its search for wisdom are all material for the healing through recollection that takes place in the pilgrimage experience of the covering and guiding cloud.

The atoning identification of blood and the incense cloud with the sacrificial death of Jesus Christ as our High Priest is to be found in the letter to the Ephesians where we read that 'Christ gave himself up for us as a fragrant offering and sacrifice to God' (Ephesians 5.2, NJB). The harrowing of hell is itself a statement of the effect of Christ's atoning sacrifice, the offering of himself as the cloud of fragrance in which as God he re-collects – collects up again – the lives of those who have suffered death.

This theme is articulated with great power and beauty by the ancient homily that is appointed in the Breviary of the Roman Catholic Church as one of the readings for the morning of Holy Saturday. The author imagines a silence over all the earth as its King sleeps in our death. Then, describing a scene that is frequently to be found in icons of the resurrection, the homily gives an account of the descent into the underworld.

Passing through the generations of his pre-history, Jesus makes his way, wielding 'his victorious weapon, the cross' to Adam and Eve. In this meeting, 'he who is God and Adam's son' recalls the experience of his Passion that in each respect is a mirror image of the story of creation and a means of restoration: 'spittle on my face . . . to restore you to that first divine inbreathing . . . blows on my cheek . . . to refashion your distorted form to my own image'. This graphic imagery (totally familiar to the imagination of the ancient world, as we know from the story of Orpheus) is an enactment of how the fragrance of life envelops the stench of death, remembering and collecting the human race into the cloud of the presence of God. The reading ends with a description of what awaits us: 'the food is provided, the everlasting houses and rooms are in readiness, the treasures of good things have been opened'.

In this reading we can perceive our death to be the emotional source of the cry, 'Forget not', from the psalmist, and we can direct that cry to the God of all time, the God who remembers as we articulate the anxiety of our post-

Christian culture, and seek to direct it to the source of consolation. This cry is heard and understood in the liturgy of the Easter Vigil by the declaration that the pillar of fire, the Easter or Paschal candle (a different manifestation, using the sense of sight, of the cloud that enfolds and leads) is the symbolic representation of Jesus Christ, in whom all our life is remembered in God. Here we understand the place of prayers for those whom we have loved and who have died. It is a statement of healing in memory and recollection, the engraving of our hope upon the risen Christ, whose symbol, the Paschal candle, attends the funeral ceremonies of our departure from this world into the rest and keeping of God.

When the Paschal candle is blessed, a definition of our time span is literally engraved upon it as a statement about the incarnate God who has died and risen again and will open to us the gates of eternity, to which the pillar of fire and cloud leads us. These are the words that are engraved, and behind them we detect the consolation for our yearning that we, and those we have loved, be not forgotten:

> Christ yesterday and today,
> the beginning and the end,
> Alpha and Omega,
> all time belongs to him,
> and all ages;
> to him be glory and power,
> through every age and for ever. Amen.
>   (from *Lent, Holy Week and Easter*)

The smell of the Sabbath

The engraving and lighting of the Easter candle in the darkness of Holy Saturday night has a liminal quality to it. The people that gather together outside their church are like those chilly exiles who disembarked after the Flood and stood on the brink of a new and bewildering world order. We, like them, light a bonfire and use it to declare our trust in the eternal covenant that is now sealed by Jesus Christ. From the blaze of this new fire, both a pillar of cloud in the offering of incense, and a pillar of light in the Paschal candle, cover and lead the people that seek the source of life guaranteed by the sacramental experience of baptism and the Eucharist. These sacraments are replete with the imagery of journeying, to which the celebration of the Easter Vigil calls us. In baptism, the sacrament of Christian enlightenment, the vision of faith by which to discern the path is bestowed, while the Eucharist provides food and refreshment for the wayfarer.

However, the way that lies ahead of us may not be an obvious one. What are we letting ourselves in for? What will the journey be like? This is a venture of exploration in which faith is our guide, but it is not necessarily the guarantee of easily made decisions, certainties about the will of God, or unquestionable codes of obedience to them.

In the tentative nature of this journeying we recognize a similar exploration to those who, like Rose Macaulay, struggle with unresolved compulsions and fear that they will find little sympathy or understanding within the institutional Church. Through the character of Laurie in *The Towers of Trebizond* Rose Macaulay describes herself as having *some* friends who are Christians. Her emotional and intellectual struggle with Christian faith and participation in the worshipping life of the Church is outlined in the collection of letters written from 1950 to 1952 between her and Father Hamilton Johnson, a priest of the Society of St John the Evangelist, popularly known as the Cowley Fathers.

In the biographical introduction to those letters, Constance Babington Smith describes how Macaulay fell in love with a man whom she subsequently discovered to be married. Throughout the 1920s the affair continued, as a result of which she gave up institutional religion. Her lover died during the Second World War; she lived on, rediscovered the practice of her faith and died in October 1958.

Today, people are perhaps more likely to have had no Christian association, but might just have *one* friend who knows someone who might be Christian. This must not obscure the sense of dislocation felt by many who search for something that is beyond the fixed horizons of a rational universe, and in this something hope to find someone who will break the cycle of self-absorption, isolation and restlessness into which we are so often locked.

The experience that Christians have of doubting the senses and challenging the intellect may be shared with others who today seek that dimension of human identity that is spiritual, often elusive, and eternal. Writing of the perception of a church as holy ground Philip Larkin notes that the quest for this experience

> . . . never can be obsolete,
> Since someone will forever be surprising
> A hunger in himself to be more serious,
> And gravitating with it to this ground,
> Which, he once heard, was proper to grow wise in,
> If only that so many dead lie around.
>
> (Collected Poems)

The 'hunger . . . to be more serious' is a phrase that could describe the award-winning film, *The Scent of a Woman*. In a bravura performance, Al Pacino plays an overbearing, able but discreetly disgraced, blind and retired Lieutenant Colonel whose daughter hires a young college lad as a minder for her father so that she can have a weekend off. Being blind, and with the artistry of military training in

resourcefulness, the Lieutenant-Colonel learns how to proceed by smell, scenting character, atmosphere, quality, and
more than a little danger and trouble by way of forbidden
recreation during his weekend away from his daughter. At
the end of the film the action turns to the concerns of the
student minder, Charlie Simms, who is accused of refusing
to identify the culprits of a prank that had brought his college, the Baird School, into disrepute, but in fact had
unmasked the superficiality and double standards of its
Principal.

The Principal arraigns Simms and a contemporary,
George Willis, before the whole college and its disciplinary
board of governors and asks the two students to reveal the
names of those responsible. George shifts his ground and
through a collection of half-truths leaves Charlie to face the
inquiry alone. Charlie refuses to reveal the names. Before
the Principal is able to request that the board expel him,
Colonel Slade speaks up.

As a blind man, Slade speaks to an inquiry about who saw
what. He speaks with the power of a different vision, one in
which his finely attuned sense of smell enables him to recollect, without sight of the distracting backdrop of privilege
and power, how it is that people twist and dissemble. He
points to Charlie's strength of character in refusing to be
bought or intimidated into snitching on those who had
revealed a moral crime in the life of a person living a double
standard. He points to the vindictive bullying and deceit of
the Principal who, in order to protect himself, will cheerfully
ruin Charlie's future and destroy his spirit. Slade, a veteran
of Vietnam, declares, 'I have been around, and I have seen. I
have seen boys like this with arms torn out and legs ripped
off. But there isn't nothing like the sight of an amputated
spirit; there is no prosthetic for that.'

This speech is powerfully delivered and it focuses our

attention to how we might proceed through and beyond our senses. The phrase 'amputated spirit' may well be a fearsomely accurate description of the way many of us live and function, even in our pilgrimage of faith. This is a statement about life that is partial and incomplete, dependent upon itself and limited by what it can earn, buy and dispose of. Alternatively, life lived within the cloud of God, represented by the overpowering smell of incense that brought the priests in the Temple to rest and immobility, undermines the system of the world that seeks guarantees and contracts, and control by our own determination.

Frank Slade, the blind man who sees more penetratingly than those with sight, exemplifies what we might mean by the risk of Christian believing. 'Faith our outward sense befriending, makes the inward vision clear': this is how St Thomas Aquinas articulates the character of our pilgrimage in his hymn for the feast of Corpus Christi. To the outward sense, life in a cloud is blindness and lack of perspective; to faith it is the context of recollection and vision.

About a century after Aquinas composed this hymn, and at about the same time as Chaucer wrote *The Canterbury Tales*, another English scribe and gifted narrator, probably in the East Midlands, and whose name we now do not know, wrote a remarkable account of the experience of faith as our guide on a journey towards wholeness and rest. The title of that treatise is *The Cloud of Unknowing*, and although it clearly bears the marks of its own time and outlook, we find within it invaluable insights into the searching and anxieties of our own day. It addresses, for example, the anxiety of relentless reference to ourselves, providing instruction on contemplation as an antidote.

In an introduction to the text of the 1961 Penguin edition, Clifton Wolters notes that contemplation is not a 'pleasant reaction to a celestial sunset, but this basic sense of

"otherness" to which the soul turns as to its home'. The experience of being directed beyond the capacity of the senses
is simply explained: 'for sometimes God will do it all himself'
(chapter 26). Restlessness is stilled, and the remorseless
endeavour to achieve is suspended in the utter refreshment
of gift motivated solely by love. 'At such a time God may, perhaps, send out a shaft of spiritual light, which pierces this
cloud of unknowing between you, and shows you some of his
secrets, of which it is not permissible or possible to speak.
Then you will feel your affection flame with the fire of his
love, far more than I can possibly say now' (chapter 26).

The Cloud of Unknowing is not an easy treatise to read,
and if you wish to do so, it may be helpful to regard it as a
collection of reflections and advice from which you draw
some phrases that will bear repeated consideration. Among
them is a comment that reminds us of the scope of God's
gifts and the mystery of the love with which they are given,
irrespective of merit. The author of the *Cloud* is in many
respects a rigorist, but not without the humility of recognition that the grace of God challenges and transforms all
things:

> It often happens that those who have sinned hideously
> and habitually come sooner to perfect contemplation
> than those who have not sinned at all. This is a merciful
> miracle of our Lord, who has given them his special grace
> . . . I truly believe that the Day of Judgement will be a
> lovely day, when God will be seen clearly, and his gifts
> too. At that Day some of those who are now despised and
> thought nothing of, because they are common sinners –
> and perhaps even some that sin horribly – shall sit most
> fittingly with the saints in his sight. (chapter 29)

This fourteenth-century author recognized in the cloud of unknowing something of the secrecy and silence of God in the mystery of redemption. On Holy Saturday, as the light dawns on the eighth day, the resurrection day, the first and only day of the new creation, the eternal Sabbath, we gather to celebrate our baptism into the cloud, into Jesus Christ. In him our sins are covered, we are united with each other in the common experience of the fragrance of the breath of God's life, and our journeying becomes the source of our rest and satisfaction, because God re-collects us.

For further reflection . . .

Worship and remembrance
The texts, symbols and gestures that we use in worship come with a history attached to them. This history is not only the story of how we first encountered and learnt of their existence; it is also a history of how they shaped the lives of those who handed them on to us, and who in turn had received them from others.

Imbued with these layers of usage, our texts, symbols and gestures have importance as part of our inheritance, but must also have an identifiable message, meaning and purpose. For the most part they are drawn from the Bible and take us back there.

- How well do you know the texts with which you regularly worship? What is the imagery and symbolism on which they draw, where does it come from, what does it convey to you?
- Exodus 25–31 and 2 Chronicles 3–6.2 give detailed accounts of the worship of the people of Israel; how many of these details do you recognize as characteristic of Christian worship?

• Just as the different stages of our life belong to who we are now, so the different aspects of the life of Jesus celebrated in the Church's seasons colour the story of his life; how do you draw these strands together, and link Christmas with Easter, Pentecost with Candlemas, the Transfiguration with Advent?

Worship and story
Central to the celebration of the Eucharist is the prayer in which we rehearse the story of creation, the birth, life, death and resurrection of Jesus Christ, and the expectation of his return in glory. Woven into this story is the narrative of our life today, both in the intercessory listing of the needs of the world, and through the offertory representation of bread and wine, and financial gift, of our life and its content.

• What story would you tell, no matter how simple, to explain the beauty of creation and our stewardship of its resources?
• What story, not necessarily a biblical one – it might be a novel or film – describes to you something of the unconditional love of God for everyone, especially those who are labelled and feel themselves excluded from the Church?
• What piece of music, poetry, play or artistic work of human creativity brings to your mind a statement about the glory of God that the use of words in ordinary human conversation seems unable to convey?

Worship and rest
The context of worship for many people is that of time snatched out of a busy week. Alternatively, it can be time filled in an empty diary of isolation and the experience of a different kind of restlessness, that of search and anxiety driven by the discomfort of loneliness.

Jesus declares himself to be master of the Sabbath (Mark 2.28), releasing it from a constrictive identity that was about forbidding things, into one that reflects the divine experience of rest and is about enjoying things.

- Why do we work? How far does work take us beyond what is necessary, into the realms of greed, status and self-serving attainment? Do these entanglements ultimately render us powerless to determine the character of our lives and relationships?
- How is your Sunday made holy by worship, or is it more fraught by trying to deal with Christian duties? How do you maintain the balance between commitment and constriction of the spirit of rest and recreation?
- What is it like when you try to be still in the presence of God?

For a group . . .

1. Scripture reading
Exodus 14.15–31: The pillar of cloud at the crossing of the Red Sea.
Matthew 16.24–17.13: The transfiguration.
In these readings the theme of the cloud emerges as a sign of transition that leads to redemption. In the Gospel the cloud is the context in which the dispensation of the Old Testament is recalled.

2. Smell and film
If yours is a church that does not use incense, this is an opportunity to explore its use and significance. Many places now use incense very simply by burning it in a brazier; you could try that in the place where you are meeting, or explore

the sensation of smell using similar methods, such as the joss sticks that belong to a different religious tradition.

If you are familiar with the use of incense, you might spend some time comparing notes on what significance you believe it has in your worship, and how you would explain it to others less familiar with that tradition.

The film, *The Scent of a Woman*, mentioned earlier in this chapter, is available on DVD, and the sequence referred to is at the end of the film. An alternative to the film sequence, as a haunting and powerful statement of recollection, is the lament by Dido, 'When I am laid in earth' from Purcell's opera, *Dido and Aeneas*.

3. Smell and recollection
Questions for discussion:
- John Betjeman describes a Norfolk church as having the smell of wood and old leather. How would you describe the smell of your church, and what images does that smell evoke?
- The smell of incense inescapably embraces everyone in the same sensation (whatever our response to it). To what extent does your congregation represent all who live within your parish? Who is not represented? How might they find their way in?
- How does your church mark moments of remembrance that matter greatly in your neighbourhood, and identify them as held in God?
- From what might you use the excuse of activity as a means of escape? How might busy-ness justify existence because fear inhibits rest and stillness before God?
- What do you think the symbolism of the Easter Vigil is all about?

Smell: Holy Saturday

Reflection

The saying will be perfected, 'Be still and know that I am God', because there will be the greatest possible sabbath – one with no evening.

And we ourselves shall be 'the seventh day', refreshed and restored by God's blessing and sanctification. There we shall see God.

This seventh day shall be our Sabbath, whose end shall come, not with the evening, but with the Lord's day, as the eighth eternal day, sanctified and made holy by the resurrection of Christ.

This day prefigures not only the eternal rest of the spirit, but also of the body.

There we shall rest and see, we shall see and love, we shall love and we shall praise. Imagine what shall be in the end-without-end. For what else is our destiny but to come to that kingdom of which there is no end?

(St Augustine, *The City of God* (XXII.30))

Sight: Easter Day

And their eyes were opened and they recognised him; but he had vanished from their sight. Then they said to each other, 'Did not our hearts burn within us as he talked to us on the road and explained the scriptures to us?'

(Luke 24.31–32, NJB)

Unlocking the drama

'Will, where is my play?' are the first words that Mr Henslowe speaks to the penniless, love-torn and time-constrained young author who lends his name to John Madden's rich and splendid comedy, *Shakespeare in Love.* In many respects, London life at the end of the sixteenth-century is not very different from today, and the reconstruction of the Globe Theatre in Southwark, opposite St Paul's, is a reminder that names and experiences familiar to the Londoners of those days are not entirely lost to us.

Today there might be Arts Council grants, but managers of the playhouses and touring theatre companies still live from hand to mouth – quite how they survive we do not know; it's a mystery. And in spite of all the advances upon the quill that should facilitate ease of composition, reproduction and the delivery of promised pages, editors and producers are still constrained to travel in person to ask, 'Where is my play, my book, my article . . . ?'

In response to Mr Henslowe's question, Shakespeare breaks unhelpfully into a half-formed love sonnet. 'No, we haven't the time for this. Talk prose. Where is my play?' 'It is all locked safe in here,' Will replies, offering comfort to Henslowe that is insubstantial in terms of time delivery. The unlocking of his lines, the revelation of his drama is what the film is all about. It is also what the opening of the tomb is all about on Easter Day; our vision of the unlocking of the lines of scripture that had foretold this event, and the unfolding of the drama that must inevitably flow from it — and of which we are part.

Theatricality can be a term that is used to suggest something contrived or insubstantial. But that is not necessarily a fair judgement of the scope of the theatre, the depth of message it is able to communicate, or the extent to which it offers a legitimate and helpful model for explaining how we experience our lives as Christians.

Writing in *The Times* during a crisis that yet again had hit one of our great artistic institutions, Benedict Nightingale observed recently that 'the theatre may be the last place where we can gather together and, helped by a few actors, construct dreams and share fancies. It will be a gymnasium for underused imaginations.' The function of liturgy is precisely that it should provide just such a gymnasium, in which the risen Jesus reveals not only his identity but also ours in a dream that constructs reality, as biblical dreams and visions always do.

Today we may find difficulty in tracing some similarity between the bright lights of theatre advertisements and the church notice board, but in fact there is remarkable similarity of purpose. In both instances they are proclaiming a time at which drama will unfold, the nature of the drama, and the names of those who will take leading roles within it. In both cases the billboards are invitatory; entry is by choice.

And although some difference in the nature of the cost involved will also determine accessibility, neither Church nor theatre can be complacent about its popular appeal.

Perhaps Shakespeare's contemporary, the Anglican divine and apologist, Richard Hooker, has in mind the impact of the billboard and the drawing of crowds to a spectacle, whether sacred or secular, when he writes about the revelation of God in the sacraments. There is something here of the billboard notification that enables the Christian to recognize specific moments of drama in which God reveals Godself in the unfolding life of sanctification. Hooker's observation comes from his description of the sacraments in his treaties *Of the Laws of Ecclesiastical Polity*. He writes:

> The Apostles by fiery tongues which they saw, were
> admonished when the Spirit, which they could not
> behold, was upon them. In like manner it is with us.
> Christ and his Holy Spirit with all their blessed effects,
> though entering into the soul of man we are not able to
> apprehend or express how, do notwithstanding give
> notice of the times when they use to make their access,
> because it pleaseth Almighty God to communicate by sen-
> sible means those blessings which are incomprehensible.

The implication here is that moments of revelatory vision are not accidental. Although it is not possible to set any limit to the way in which God communicates with us ('entering into the soul of man we are not able to apprehend or express how'), nonetheless there are moments, places and materials ('sensible means') by which we are assured of the disclosure of the presence of God. These 'sensible means' are what we speak of as the sacraments, and Hooker is clear that grace is communicated through them by sight, but also by more than that. They are not 'bare resemblances' or 'naked signs' for us merely to enjoy looking at; they are moral instruments that command our obedience as within them we meet the Saviour of all.

The point being made here is that the drama of the liturgy, itself the notification of the time in which the grace of God is communicated, commands our participation not only in its formal processes, but also in the manner by which we live out our lives. The boundaries between the stage, the world and eternity are suspended. We discover that Jesus is not remote, the person on the stage or the spectacle we have come to see: he incorporates us into his body of players.

In an article about sacramentality, the French theologian Louis-Marie Chauvet describes the medieval understanding of Jesus as the author/actor of the sacraments. It is an interesting reference, since subsequent to the period that he describes we find the emergence of the Mystery Plays that made a huge impact upon the lives and spiritual imagination of the people of Europe. These para-liturgical mission presentations combined the spoken word of scripture and the liturgical shape of sacrament and tradition in order to give expression to the Christian faith through the popular medium of drama and enacted symbol.

But the apparent acceptance by the Church of the worth of the medieval Mystery Plays that are now re-enacted in York Minster, for example, was not easily won. Although the intention was 'to instruct the populace in those truths essential for their salvation by rendering them accessible, and to alert men and women to the cosmic battles being waged over the fate of their own immortal and individual souls', nonetheless there was also suspicion of the way in which the theatre revealed these mysteries.

One of the great international theologians of the last century, Hans Urs von Balthasar, gives to the second part of his theological trilogy the title Theo-drama. In the Introduction, von Balthasar considers the history of drama in the celebration and expression of the Christian life, and identifies something of the unease that we might sense in dealing with the term 'theatricality'. He notes the Church's 'uncritically accepted tradition' of 'promoting and admiring the work of artists whom, at the same time, it cast out from its midst'. As recently as the nineteenth century, clergy in Paris were forbidden to go to public theatres or the opera, and in the latter part of that century, the Christian Socialist priest, Stewart Headlam, was disciplined by his bishop, Frederick Temple, for promoting interest in the ballet and the cause of women who worked in the music halls of London.

But as the title in von Balthasar's trilogy suggests, there is more to the place of drama in the Christian tradition than simply its history. Drama is a statement of revelation and conviction, a means by which we see and participate in an enacted symbol that discloses the transforming effect and claim of something that cannot be seen. In the context of Christian life this would mean that what we hear and see in church, the proclamation of the word of God and the breaking of bread at the altar, and what we experience in prayer, study and reflection as a means of personal encounter with God, both find enhanced significance in the dramatic experience of the gathered Church in worship.

Von Balthasar puts it in these terms: 'The theatrical element adds a further, perhaps more hidden aspect: the thought that here something is being acted out for me awakens the deeper realization that everything that has taken place is "for me"; it happened on my account and so ultimately has a claim on me.' This is a disturbing perception, for it turns the spotlight upon us. No longer can we remain safely at a distance to invest in others the responsibility for the production and action of the play; now we are implicated. Life and drama coalesce.

The spectacle of our lives

Part of the attraction of *Shakespeare in Love* is its weaving together of a story that combines life and drama so as to illuminate both. Will falls in love with the beautiful Lady Viola, who is betrothed to Lord Wessex but so captivated by the young playwright that she disguises herself as a boy, Thomas Kent, in order to be able to join his players. A hasty and forced marriage intercepts her plans. However, she slips away from her wedding breakfast in order to witness the play Will has written for and about her, and she is asked to stand in at the last moment for the lead role, that of Juliet. But at the end of the play – and the film – the intervention of the Chamberlain and the force of law that forbids women to act in the playhouse reveals Viola's true identity, and both Lord Wessex and the Queen, Elizabeth I, are present to witness it.

Settling accounts outside the playhouse, the Queen colludes with the transformation of identities that the playhouse had made possible. She sends 'Master Kent' back into it to deliver the profits of a wager to Will Shakespeare, and to 'send out' Lady Viola Wessex, who will set sail with her new husband to his tobacco plantations in America. But the transformation is more complex: this Lady Viola will become another character, Viola, in *Twelfth Night* and perpetuate our speculation as to the identity of the muse who unlocked the lines in Shakespeare's head.

In this example, it is the players in the film who act out for us the scope of transformation that becomes possible in the theatre, and the boundary that it calls into question between the world into which it has invited us to leap and exercise our imagination, and the reality of our lives that we confront in that gymnasium and beyond it. Two gospel stories of the resurrection invite us to discern a similar kind of experience.

On the journey to Emmaus, Jesus (the author/actor) raises the curtain on the drama when he joins Cleopas and his companion on the road out of Jerusalem. He is acting out his role within the framework of the story, entering into the drama of non-recognition by his companions, even though they fall into a detailed discussion about his identity. They reach the village, and the play unfolds in a meal for which Jesus had prepared their hearts and minds so that their imaginations were able to make the leap from a familiar and routine series of gestures to recognition of the resurrection. We might say that in the theatre of the breaking of bread they saw Jesus risen from the dead, a vision (dream-like, but more than a dream) that so reconstructed their perspective of reality as to make new sense of everything else about their lives and experience.

This is the context of theatre in which transformation takes place and it is similarly played out in the encounter with Mary Magdalen in John's Gospel. Here again, Jesus acts out the role of mistaken identity that is required of him. The role that Jesus takes on is in itself highly significant, and adds new layers of symbolism to the drama, since as the gardener he is understood as the true husbandman who works upon the neglected garden of our hearts and souls. In a homily attributed to St Macarius, the background to the persona of this character is described: 'He pulled up the thorns and thistles of evil spirits and tore up the weeds of sin . . . When thus he had tilled the ground of the soul with the wooden plough of his cross, he planted in it a lovely garden of the Spirit.'

Jesus plays out the role of gardener in a deepening of the dramatic symbolism and to prepare for the revelation that will come in a moment of pure theatricality; the speaking of one word: her name. The drama of that moment is virtually impossible to capture in any liturgical reading of the story, but we surely have no difficulty in understanding the depth and power of the emotion that it releases as it establishes a new level of relationship between Jesus and Mary and deepens the transformation of her character as one who builds penitence into witness and apostolate.

At this point we should remind ourselves of the observation by von Balthasar that in the drama of Christian celebration we are not neutral observers, but, inescapably, participants, as we begin to recognize that everything 'happened on my account and so ultimately has a claim on me'. Here, we reach the point of fundamental difference between liturgy and secular theatre. In the playhouses of today we might experience many profound and life-changing moments, but the transformation is dependent upon private judgement and experience, expressed and further explored beyond the context of the audience, the other people with whom a particular play has been witnessed.

In the secular playhouse there is nothing that requires of us any relationship with each other. There is no exchange of a sign of peace. We are highly unlikely ever to meet again. And when the play has ended, the players return to being other people; the beautiful duchess is to be seen queuing in McDonald's for a late-night Big Mac and fries, the ruthless millionaire smokes roll-ups, has holes in his jeans and cannot afford a decent push-bike. And we go home. No matter how close the action comes to us personally, it cannot ultimately have a claim upon us collectively. That is not so in the playhouse of God. This is where we see the truth about ourselves played out in ways that take our confusions from where they are to a disclosure that transfigures mistaken identity into deeper truth, and we discover that we, the audience, are also the players. When the action of the drama, which is liturgical, ceases, we continue to be what we have become in that transformative arena. The last line

Known to the Senses

of the play, 'Go, in the peace of Christ', is the first line of the rest of the action for which each of us is responsible.

Cleopas and his companion go back to Jerusalem to continue the drama by informing the other disciples. Mary Magdalen enters upon the stage of apostolic vocation with the stunning line, 'I have seen the Lord.' And such is the nature of the vision of God that the Magdalen consequently secures in our imagination and art a transformation of character that exemplifies moral and physical beauty redeemed. And what of us? What do we do? How do we undertake the action of witness and mission as players of the Gospel?

So much of the answer to that question depends upon the unique configuration of gifts that God has given each of us. But the answer also holds within it the possibility that God will surprise us with the discovery of gifts that makes us ideally suited for our role in a particular place and time. Above all, the task of being one of the players is not beyond what we are capable of being, nor is it a distortion of ourselves.

In his *Meditations on the Priestly Life*, the Jesuit theologian, Karl Rahner, made a wise observation that applies to all Christians; that we must be convincing as human beings. This does not imply conformity to the world, 'but it implies that the person who meets us has the chance to see that being a Christian is not something contrary to basic human feelings'. A good place to begin with the playing-out of the role entrusted to us in the playhouse of the Church is the small dramas of home, street, work and neighbourhood. At an essential level of human decency there is much to be defended and supported in the formation of our society in which we are charged with promoting values that reflect the society of the kingdom of heaven. Here is one small example.

At least a decade ago, a member of my congregation who, like many others, was a grandmother, a widow and a member of the Mothers' Union, used to wear on her lapel the red ribbon that indicated support of AIDS sufferers. Eventually I asked her about the ribbon. She wore it because the people who lived next door to her were gay; many of their friends had died of AIDS, others were HIV-positive. In the early days of her widowhood and grief these neighbours had been among her most supportive friends and she had grown to respect and love them.

She was not a campaigning sort of person who easily espoused causes, but she believed in respect, deplored prejudice, and confidently trusted that no one was beyond the love of God. It was a strong faith, simple and profound. She may never have spoken to anyone else about her ribbon. But through it she played her part in making a statement about her faith that understood basic human feelings to be the compass that points us to the truth of God.

In Leicester, where I was a curate, that level of respect for human dignity, and confidence in the love of God, was widely evident among our congregations. It fostered an understanding with the Hindu Asian community among whom we lived as Christians that made me proud to be identified as one of the priests who served in that area. But we also had much to learn from our Hindu neighbours about the value of the external expressions of faith. Not only in the dramatic worship and devotions in the local temple, a place that daily attracted a more regular stream of devotees than, I suspect, any of the City churches, but also in their houses, the signs of devotion were enacted. They played their part in living the Hindu life in ways that cohered with their cultural identity and basic human feelings.

When overwhelming levels of tension between East and West threaten the stability of society that is multi-faith and multi-racial, a part that we as Christians have to play is the circulation on our street of the currency of respect for human dignity, tolerance and trust in the love of God who gives us the earth as the statement of divine hospitality. The extension of that currency of hospitality to others is nothing less than our duty. The danger that befalls us when that currency is withdrawn into our own savings accounts is graphically illustrated by the well-known words of Pastor Martin Niemöller preached in a post-war sermon in the USA:

> In Germany they first came for the communists and
> I didn't speak up because I wasn't a communist. Then
> they came for the Jews, and I didn't speak up because
> I wasn't a Jew. Then they came for the trade unionists,
> and I didn't speak up because I wasn't a trade unionist.
> Then they came for the Catholics, and I didn't speak up
> because I was a Protestant. Then they came for me –
> and by that time no one was left to speak up.

Niemöller lived through the period of Nazi Germany as a patriot and a pacifist. Eventually they did come for him and he was imprisoned for his faith. The spectacle of his life was set on a stage that was starkly drawn in black and white, imposing a segregation upon the human race that dissolved individuality in the character of those exalted on one side, at the incomprehensible expense of eradicating the dignity and life of millions who were lost on the other. Today we delude ourselves if we imagine that it is possible to relegate the inhuman contrasts of that staging to a distant drama in the past.

Half a century ago the spectacle of the Holocaust conjured up images of catastrophe that hauntingly evoke scenes of contemporary drama in which we are internationally participants, not spectators:

104

Sight: Easter Day

Never shall I forget that smoke . . .
Never shall I forget those flames . . .
Never shall I forget those mountains which murdered my
God and my soul and turned my dreams into dust.

(Ellie Weisel, *Night*)

Smoke, flames and dust are still the props with which we enact the drama of war and terrorism. They rob us of life and of colour. They consume human individuality and turn us into victims and perpetrators. They numb our imagination, and they are the staging on which so much of our life is today played out. They are the twin towers of the World Trade Centre and Baghdad, Rwanda, Darfur and the Sudan, Gaza and Jerusalem, and wherever the first suicide bomb carries that drama into the life of Western Europe.

However, the dust to which the smoke and flames reduce all that we are and are capable of being is the dust in which we are also called to write and honour words of faith and hope that must be heard above the clamour for hatred and revenge. And more than words are expected of us. The liturgy of our worship should have taught us that we learn our words of faith, prayer and adoration in order to be able to perform our multiple parts in the mission to reveal the spectacle of the kingdom of God. Our medium is drama, unfolded through lives transformed by participation in the vision of what lies beyond the curtain.

The spectacle of God
It is, perhaps, a helpful accident that in the design of the theatres of the nineteenth and early twentieth centuries, the raising of the curtain heralds the beginning of the drama. This action evokes the statement in Matthew's Gospel that the veil of the Temple was torn in two from top to bottom (Matthew 27.51). It also takes us into the

language and drama of the letter to the Hebrews, to the reminder that Jesus has, once for all, enacted with eternal significance the atoning ministry of the High Priest, making 'a living opening through the curtain, that is to say, his flesh' (Hebrews 10.20, NJB). In this curtain symbolism, we find an important detail about the vision and spectacle of the drama of our lives.

Scriptural references to the curtain of the Temple indicate that it was 'of violet, scarlet, crimson and fine linen' with a 'design of winged creatures on it' (2 Chronicles 2.14; Exodus 26.31, NJB). This curtain defined the Holy of Holies, the place where God was understood to dwell in pure light. The colour of the curtain was a statement about the refraction of the unity of light into the multiplicity of colour as an expression of the majesty of God. Our flesh and blood is an expression of that refraction; that is why it makes sense to speak of the multiple colours of the curtain as the flesh of Jesus at the moment when that flesh is torn in death and he is reunited with the life-giving Father in whom all things are one. And this connects us with another scriptural convention about the vision of those who dwell in heaven: the white robe.

When Jesus is transfigured on Mount Tabor, the detail on which all three Evangelists that narrate this event are agreed is the description of his clothing – its dazzling whiteness as the evidence of his heavenly identity. This is a convention that draws on the book of Daniel and its vision of the Son of Man ('his clothing was white as snow', Daniel 7.9, NRSV) and the imagery of the Revelation of John, in which those who are gathered around the throne and of the Lamb are described as dressed in white robes (Revelation 7.9). White, as dazzling as the brightness of light, is a metaphor for the unity of heaven, from whence light refracted through the prism of creation is dispersed into the colours of the spectrum.

All the glory that is contained in the amazing dispensation of colour is drawn together to express in the symbolic garments of white robes this phenomenon of visual and chromatic unity from multiplicity. In Revelation the vision of heaven does not deny the existence of colour. It paints the heavenly Jerusalem in the most vivid colours imaginable, enumerated through the precious stones that form its foundations and walls (Revelation 21.18–20) in order to emphasize the dynamic of unity that white robes represent. In the drama that we use to enact our points of union with heaven, colour is a vital symbol, expressing the glory of God in creation, and our identity as those in whom creation is perfected, brought into unity, so that ultimately we see our glorious colour in pure light.

The drama of movement between light and colour is something that we see explored in art and enacted in liturgy. In almost all worship the lighting of candles has a part. In whatever form it happens, the visual impact of the use of light is a statement about the perfection and unity of God, and in the use of a flame there is a clear and powerful statement about light that lives and moves, indeed, that dances – itself a form of drama that is used to describe the life of God.

Similarly, the wearing of vestments of regulated colour over white robes is a statement of the dynamic relationship between unity and heaven (white) and multiplicity and creation (colour) that articulates the majesty of God revealed in Jesus who plays out the drama of our life and birth and adds the new beginning of resurrection. From the unity of light in the eternal Trinity he who is the beloved of the Father comes forth into the visible polychromatic glory of flesh, through which he returns to unity by way of redemption and in the Spirit draws all things into that same light and unity.

This cycle of revelation – redemption – return is often well expressed in art form. Among the huge canvases of

El Greco the interplay between the zones on heaven and earth is powerfully captured. 'The Burial of the Count of Orgaz', for example, depicts the legend of the appearance, gloriously apparelled, of St Stephen and St Augustine to bury the godly Count whose soul is seen being carried to Christ who is clothed in white and seated in glory.

This vast painting presents the framework for a drama about the ashen absence of colour in death, the vitality of the manifestation of colour as a statement of creation redeemed, and the unity of light from which Jesus sheds upon us new life. The connections between earth and heaven are to be seen first in the drama of a life of generosity and humility lived by the Count in discipleship of Jesus his Lord; second in the communion of saints who recognize the lifestyle of a kindred disciple and so descend to welcome him into their company; and finally in the experience of death at which we take our leave of the ashes of exile and are welcomed into the glory of resurrection.

The Evangelists record the angels who attest the resurrection, and the transfiguration of Jesus that had foreshadowed it, as characterized by dazzling light and the brilliance of the white vesture. These statements do not invalidate our experience of, or existence in, colour. When we speak of vision, we think of a medium that is in colour. If we do not see the colour, we sense that some part of our vision is impaired. Nor is light or whiteness the opposite or denial of colour. We think of a white page or a blank screen of light as empty because we have no other means for registering the absence of creativity and life. But in the metaphorical language and imagery that we use of God, these are statements that indicate not absence but abundance, to a degree of richness and intensity that our senses are incapable of comprehending.

In the Preface to his book, *Mystical Theology*, Mark

McIntosh introduces his impressive exploration of the relationship between theology and spirituality by telling a story about what would happen if

> all the artists of the world suddenly went colour-blind. Their works would continue to be marvels of structure and movement, but the rest of us 'amateurs' would constantly feel that the artists had lost touch with something vital, that some mysterious language for expressing the vitality of the real had been forgotten.

The loss of the mystical language of the senses and imagination is something to which life in drama, art and colour recall us as media without which we are unable to speak of God in ways that emanate from our deepest soul and experience.

Our discourse about God becomes self-contained and theoretical if disconnected from the vision of lives lived sacrificially and joyfully in the fullest richness of our humanity. We become victims of the world's boredom if we collude with its manipulation of our diversity and colour into the patterns of its own sameness and conformity. The notion of what is mystical, however, is not to be equated with mythical mystification or esoteric individualism. The mystical element of Christianity absorbs colour and the social media of the dramatic arts and imagination, and in conjunction with the words, reason and coherence of our written lines (theology), gives us the opportunity to employ the full content of our faith in mission.

Conformity to the values of the world has a colour determined by death: it is the colour of dust and ash. But our evangelistic mission must be driven by knowledge that there is also colour. We have seen it; it is beautiful. Nothing can ever be the same again. And this is an experience we must share with others, because we see colour in them as well. John O'Donohue, in *The Way* No. 34, describes this evangelistic task as an awakening, as though for the first time we see beyond black and white, beyond isolation, dust and ash, into the colour of the creative weave of the Trinity 'where Being is Belonging, where memory transfigures transience, where death changes into divine life and where time is but eternity living dangerously'.

Critically for us, experience of the transfiguration that drives our evangelism is not derived solely from the recognition of what this feels like to us. It is driven, also, by the vision of what has happened in God, a drama that is narrated in the pages of the scriptures.

In a poem about this drama, entitled 'Rublev', Archbishop Rowan Williams captures something of the multi-faceted nature of its entanglements. It is a story about giving, and the life of the Trinity is a good place in which to start. Elsewhere the Archbishop describes the unfolding of the drama of the Trinity like this: 'God gives God, having nothing else to give . . . The Father, in eternally giving (divine) life to the Son, gives that life as itself a "giving" agency [God the Spirit]'. But then there is also what we give to God, and the only thing that we have is the life and creation God has given us, mangled and marred by our usage of it. This is where the colour comes in.

The poem, is a meditation on how the Russian icon writer found the inspiration for his vision of God the Trinity. It was the vision of an encounter that arose out of the brutal drama of human existence, as the colour scheme illustrates.

> One day, God walked in, pale from the grey steppe,
> slit-eyed against the wind, and stopped,
> said, Colour me, breathe your blood into my mouth.

Sight: Easter Day

I said, Here is the blood of all our people,
these are their bruises, blue and purple,
gold, brown, and pale green wash of death.

These (god) are the chromatic pains of flesh,
I said, I trust I make you blush,
O I shall stain you with the scars of birth.

For ever. I shall root you in the wood,
under the sun shall bake you bread
of beechmast, never let you forth

To the white desert, to the starving sand.
But we shall sit and speak around
one table, share one food, one earth.

Where Rublev leaves off, Caravaggio picks up. The table,
food and earth that Jesus shares with Emmaus companions
after his resurrection is our Eucharist and the location in
which drama breaks into reality, colour dissolves into light,
dust and ash are transfigured into life eternal.

For further reflection . . .

Seeing and performing
Soap operas fascinate us because they present ordinary life
as drama. We appear to feature in or near what they portray. There should be a similar fascination in the drama of
the liturgy that depends on its visual impact and closeness
to something transcendent that it is not easy to put into
words. Even when worship is not liturgical, it is often presented very skilfully on a plasma screen, exploiting all the
drama of the visual and evoking something more than the
immediate and obvious.

- To what extent does the experience of participation in the liturgy stir your imagination?
- How do you register and express your actual participation to its fullest potential?
- How would you describe to someone else the many levels at which the drama of the liturgy is celebrated?
- If you have ever seen worship being relayed simultaneously on screen, how did that change the visual impact and sense of what was happening?

Seeing and believing

Jesus commends those who, unlike Thomas the twin, believe without seeing. The visual appearance of Jesus in his resurrection body has a corporal reality about it. Subsequent to the Ascension that reality is hidden from us, no matter how firm our faith.

Today we live in a culture that is more dependent than ever on the impact of the visual. We are mesmerized by image and fashion, to the extent that it can make it difficult for us to be ourselves; and difficult to be witnesses to something that we have not seen as such, and cannot show others, although they can see the symptoms of conviction in us.

- What is the first thing that you would want people to see in you? At what point might they discover that you are a Christian?
- How would you use the sense of sight to explain and encourage exploration of the Christian faith for someone who knows nothing about it? What would you encourage that person to look for or at?
- What do you see in other people?

Sight: Easter Day

Seeing in colour

The poem 'Rublev' by Rowan Williams paints God in the colours of our life and of our death. This is a statement that links the incarnation and the cross as events in God, and it says something profound about the way in which an icon is a window that we do not look at, but through.

An icon is written with solid materials that are ground, mixed and formed into a paint by the writer. The texture of the paint is determined by the use to which it is applied; rough texture for painting grass or buildings, smooth for silk or fine linen. Thus the colours of creation become the intelligible means of discernment that enables us to look into eternity as the blinding colour of pure light.

- What is your favourite painting or icon, and what does it say to you about your faith?
- Jesus, famously, says to Mary Magdalen, 'Do not cling to me' (John 20.17, NJB). To what extent do we believe that what we see is real? How does seeing have a transformative effect?
- Easter marks our renewal in mission. As St Paul began his renewal and conversion with a blinding vision of the risen Christ in the colour of pure light, how ready are you to move beyond where the senses guide, into knowledge of God that strips us of control and demands naked faith?

For a group . . .

1. Scripture reading

Daniel 7.8–14: The vision of the Son of Man in heaven.

John 20.11–29: The vision of the risen Son of Man.

These readings present us with different types of vision, and the demand for interpretation, expressed in the conventions of Old Testament apocalyptic (drawing aside the curtain)

and a more modern style of scepticism articulated by the
apostle Thomas.

2. Perception and film

The group might meet in church, if it is a building that is
rich in Christian iconography, and explore what images of
the resurrection there are and how effectively they express
some statement about our new life in Christ. If that is not
appropriate, each person could bring a postcard, icon, object
of devotion and explain what one might see in it.

The final scenes from *Shakespeare in Love*, described
earlier in this chapter, could also be used to provoke a discussion about identity, how we accurately or mistakenly
perceive it in others, how we act it out ourselves, and what
motivates us. Similar issues are raised by Mike Leigh's
insightful comedy, *Secrets and Lies*. In an early sequence a
young, professional black woman, Hortense, is given the file
on her adoption; she subsequently learns that her birth
mother is white. Both films are available on DVD.

3. Unlocking the drama

Questions for discussion:

- How good are your billboards? Do they accurately and
  attractively communicate the notice of the times when
  God will communicate through sensible means what is
  incomprehensible?
- What place does drama have in your communication of
  the gospel? If it is restricted to the liturgy, how good is
  that as drama, by its own standards and those of what is
  possible today?
- Theatre at its best grips basic human feelings. Does your
  celebration and communication of the Christian faith
  engage every part of what it means to be human?
- We are tragically aware that people will give their own

lives for vengeful purposes, too often resulting in death, dust and ash. How well prepared are we as Christians to model an alternative lifestyle, of joyful sacrifice for peaceful and life-giving purposes?

· What is your Easter message, in no more than 25 words? (Do *not* make this a committee activity!)

Reflection

With what procrastinations dost thou wait, my soul,
since thou canst even now love God in thy heart?

Mine are the heavens and mine is the earth;
Mine are the people, the righteous are mine
and mine are the sinners;
The angels are mine and the Mother of God
and all things are mine;
And God Himself is mine and for me,
for Christ is mine and all for me.
What, then, dost thou ask for and see, my soul?
All this is thine, and it is all for thee.
Consider not thyself as mean, neither pay heed
to the crumbs which fall from thy Father's table.

Go thou forth from them and glory in thy glory.

Hide thee therein and rejoice
And thou shalt have the desires of thy heart.

(From 'A Prayer of the Soul Enkindled with Love',
St John of the Cross)

Known to the Senses